Along My Line

D1627363

This specially prepared edition, issued in 1955, is for members of The Popular Book Club, 9 Long Acre, London, W.C.2, from which address particulars of membership will gladly be sent. This volume is published by arrangement with Putnam & Co. Ltd., the original publishers

GILBERT HARDING

Along My
Line

THE POPULAR BOOK CLUB

LONDON

MADE AND PRINTED IN GREAT BRITAIN
THE POPULAR BOOK CLUB (ODHAMS PRESS LTD.)
BY ODHAMS (WATFORD) LIMITED,
WATFORD, HERTS
S.255.SCP

ILLUSTRATIONS

*To Mother
who deserved so much more
and so much better*

AUTHOR'S PREFACE

IF a man must write his autobiography—and in most cases there is little enough reason why he should do so—he should at least enjoy a modicum of seclusion. He owes it as much to his readers as to himself. Reflection, self-examination and tranquillity are necessities for this task. It almost amounts to bad manners to address the reader without them.

This is the one apology I have to make. There has been no tranquillity. These pages have been written amid the stress of an active public life from which there is little or no escape. It is a story put together with many interruptions and many breaks at a period of my life when I have been constantly on the move. For this unintentional, but to me distressing, breach of manners, I will ask forgiveness in advance—but for nothing else.

Let me take this opportunity of acknowledging the assistance of my friend Charles Hamblett, poet and journalist, in many matters relating to the production of this work and to the patience of the publishers to whom I have been a more than ordinary nuisance.

GILBERT HARDING

1

On Wednesday, June 5, 1907, Orby won the Derby and I was born in the Union Workhouse, Hereford. I arrived about an hour before the "off." My father was Master there, my mother the Matron. She was attended at my delivery by the sick bay's superintendent nurse, Miss Cork—as in bottle.

There is something very peculiar—and quite damning to the ego—about being brought up in a workhouse as the child of the Master and Matron. There are lots of people who call you Master Gilbert and wait on you. You never see your mother engaged in domestic work because there are so many folk around to make beds, clean shoes, fetch and carry. So you get the feeling that you are somebody, and unless that feeling is carefully corrected by mother and father, it can be very dangerous. When you get outside the workhouse and start growing up away from that environment, you find that you are not some kind of princeling after all. Indeed, you learn that children of workhouse officials are regarded as little better than the pauper inmates. Socially, you are classed as inferior to the sons of small tradesmen and clerks—especially when it is realized that the rates those people pay help to keep you, along with the paupers, in comfort; an item which they are not slow to point out!

My first five years laid the foundation of everything that followed. In the gracious gardens and scrupulously spick-and-span rooms of the family domain, I soon acquired a quite spurious sense of grandeur, despite the fact (which I did not then know) that my parents' joint income amounted to £90 a year. There I was, conscious of my parents' very real love for me, strutting about the garden with its fine lawns and fascinating corners, its pear trees and rows and rows of kidney beans, my imagination unchecked, my wanderings uncurbed, free as a bird and happy as a king.

In one far corner of the garden was a most wonderful sandpit where I acted out my fantasies of command. I was a pirate chief, an explorer, a general leading my troops to victory—always to victory. (Like Napoleon, I did not learn— till it was too late—the meaning of defeat.) Then, when the sand gave out and the pit became a rubbish dump, it was even more exciting. There I was, a proud little chanticleer, crowing on my dustheap.

My parents were always good to me. I remember Father as a quiet, kindly man. My chief recollection was of his gentle remonstrance when, like him, I attempted to call my mother by her Christian name. "Never," he said, taking me aside, "never again let me hear you refer to your mother as May. *I* call her May. *You* call her Mummy." How right he was to insist on wholesome domestic convention!

Father, quite unlike me, was universally esteemed. This may seem a paradox, considering he was a Workhouse Master at a time when Oliver Twist could still have been one of his more elderly inmates. He was a 'good companion' with a host of friends and the gift of making the unfortunate paupers accept his authority without their suffering any sense of degradation. In those early days of the present century, poor folk were still expected, as that ugly Victorian cliché has it, "to know their place." Though by no means a revolutionary, or even a progressive father, he did consider other people's human feelings.

I come, by the way, from workhouse officials on both sides of the family. My mother's father, Charles King, was the son of a Buckinghamshire farm labourer. He was a bright little boy and received more schooling than most village lads at that time. During the 1870s he took a job in the Poor Law Service at Aylesbury Workhouse. He then went to the old Princess Road Institution—long since pulled down—in Lambeth where he met Ruth Boyce who came from Thetford

10

in Norfolk. She was fourteen years his senior but they married in 1885, applied for the job of Master and Matron at Hereford Union Workhouse and arrived there with their three daughters, the middle of whom was May, my mother.

I do not know how my father's father, Gilbert William Harding, and his wife, Mary Priscilla, came to be joint superintendents of the Children's Home at Caerleon-upon-Usk, but they did so and there they brought into the world a large family of whom my father, also Gilbert, was the eldest.

He, too, had a better education than many in his station at that time, going to Derby School as a choral scholar. Early in the nineteen-hundreds he went to Hereford as assistant schoolmaster in the workhouse, under my Grandfather King. There he met and fell in love with my mother. Since their past was linked, they decided that their future might just as well be, and to that end they studied diligently. My mother went to Leeds to train as a nurse and by the time my father had qualified for the job, it was time for the Kings to retire. So Mr. and Mrs. Harding became Master and Matron at Hereford.

As I grew up I became aware of someone like an intruder in my little world, another claimant to my parents' affection. This was my sister, Constance, a year older than I—and always years older in common sense. I do not now remember what demon prompted our incessant quarrels, but one day I went too far. We were sitting at table during a meal when something Constance said so infuriated me that I threw a fork at her. It cut the flesh just above the left eye. A more stupid woman than my mother would no doubt have inflicted some physical vengeance on me. All she did in fact was to order me to my room. There I was left alone, and—as is always my way after I have behaved badly—remorse overcame me. I knew I had done wrong and awaited my punishment. When it came, I was mystified. At breakfast the following morning my father handed me a spoon—and no fork. For months I was obliged to eat everything with this spoon. I have hated physical violence ever since.

11

Quite early in life I formed a violent dislike of old Grandfather King. A harsh, pompous, vain man, he and his wife lived in a small villa (later my mother's home) about a mile away. One day my mother took me to visit a Mr. Cooper at Ross, some fourteen miles away. Mr. Cooper gave me a fine plucked chicken to take home. I remember the delight I felt on the way home, carrying my chicken. When we got back, there was my grandfather waiting to take the chicken back to his villa. I was furious. Mr. Cooper had given the chicken to me. Grandfather had no right to the bird. The old man, on the contrary, argued that Cooper was his friend and that he considered the chicken as *his* gift. Taking it from me, he stalked off in a huff. I never forgave him for depriving me of my gift.

My childhood friends were the people of the workhouse. Even after all these years I remember them as some of the kindliest people I have ever known. There was a Miss Pugh, a lady blessed with a noble voice, who sometimes read to me when not engaged in her duties as the workhouse laundress. On the occasion of one of my many childhood illnesses (I seem to have run the gamut of ailments before my tenth year, including a number which I am sure are not listed in the medical books) I had to spend hours in bed, under some sort of improvised tent, inhaling from a steam kettle. I knew I was fairly ill (it turned out to be a touch of pneumonia) and remember upsetting my mother by asking for Miss Pugh to come to my bedside and sing "Abide with Me," a touch of the flamboyant which I suspect was deliberate.

Dr. Lilley, who always attended me, was an impressive Victorian figure. He would arrive in a wonderful shining horse carriage driven by a coachman with a cockade in his hat. The doctor himself always wore a frock coat and a top hat as shiny and polished as the sides of his magnificent equipage. As I lay in bed I would always know when the doctor was due for he was also the visiting doctor to the workhouse. So whenever he arrived the great bell of the institution would solemnly ring to warn the superintendent nurse that he was on his way and to prepare the inmates who required his attention. This I found extremely useful, for when I was getting better and wanted to "mike," I would work myself into a state of high agitation as soon as the bell began to ring and the doctor would find me sufficiently feverish to recommend another day or two in bed.

There was another great friend who would often read to me. This was an old lady who periodically sought refuge in the workhouse from what must have been an extremely arduous existence on a nearby farm. Her name was Mrs. Cohen and she was housekeeper to an equally old and extremely irascible farmer. Every now and then she would tire of her cantankerous master and come to the workhouse for a rest. When she felt sufficiently recovered she would return to the farm, to my great regret, for she had a truly lovely reading voice. Indeed, she could even make *Ivanhoe* sound interesting.

At that time, my mother has recently told me, my photographic memory, as she called it, was a great nuisance to her. She gave up reading and reciting nursery rhymes to me long before most mothers do, for I had the irritating habit of correcting her when she misread or forgot a word. Mrs. Cohen, apparently, did not suffer from my pernicketiness; otherwise I am sure I would have driven the poor woman back to the nagging farmer long before she was ready to leave her workhouse sanctuary.

Mrs. Tranter, my parents' personal charwoman, was another familiar figure of my childhood. Working through the week from seven in the morning till five in the evening, and one o'clock on Saturdays, she received ten shillings a week and her dinners for her services. For this she kept our quarters spotlessly tidy. This patient soul, whom we used to call "Tray," had a passion for polish. Everything shone. She cleaned shoes until you really could see your face in them; and she never minded how often I trudged in from the garden. Tray would simply snatch my muddy shoes from my feet and retire to a corner to resume her polishing.

Then there was dear old Granny Lewis who lived to a great age. She had a touch with a smoothing iron that was absolutely miraculous. When my grandfather—reinstalled at the workhouse for a tragic reason about which I will write shortly—went off to his Freemason's "do's," everyone (except me) would swarm around him. His shirt, still warm from the meticulous ironing of Granny Lewis, would be handed to him by his wife while in another room Tray would be brushing his coat. I remember how he would draw himself up before a mirror to scrutinize the results of these ministrations. I later saw actors doing this before making their stage entrances. In his Masonic regalia I thought he merely looked silly; but I kept my own counsel.

Grandfather was always down on me. Whenever I made any remark he would try to squash me. One day he discovered that I was being given some chocolates as a treat after breakfast. He promptly stopped this. "No more till after ten," he said sternly.

I waited till he had gone, then called for Tray. "What can I do for you, Master Gilbert?" she asked.

"Tray," I commanded, "stand on that chair over there and see if you can reach the clock on the wall." The good old soul looked somewhat alarmed but did as I bid.

"Now unclasp the catch at the side and open the glass over the clockface," I said. Tray did so.

"Now tell me what time it is," I went on.

"Eight-fifteen, Master Gilbert."

"Well, push the hands on to ten o'clock," I told her. The bewildered Tray did this and snapped the glass back.

"Now give me that box of chocolates," I said as soon as she had clambered down from the chair. On being handed the box I began to help myself. No doubt I gorged myself—I cannot remember—though my mother recalls the incident well, more especially the rumpus my grandfather created when he found out. Mother tells me all this happened shortly after my third birthday.

One day a visitor, in the presence of my grandfather, said: "Say what you like about the lad, but you must admit that he nearly always blurts out exactly what we would have liked to have said ourselves." Grandfather was not amused. Only a short while before he had overheard me telling Mother exactly what I thought of him.

Perhaps it was to avoid my grandfather—who at all times kept his eye on what went on in the workhouse—that I cultivated so many friends among the inmates. There was Nat, a cheery little man who looked after the pigs. One morning he blew up a pig's bladder, tied it to a stick, and gave it to me to play with. I ran happily about the garden, swiping at butterflies with my fool's balloon, till my grandfather caught me and confiscated the bladder.

Then there was a one-legged man called Nick, who told wonderful stories of smuggling and piracy and daring deeds on the Spanish Main. Whenever I see copies of the Millais painting, "The Boyhood of Raleigh," the sly old seadog in that painting reminds me vividly of Nick. He would yarn for hours, telling me of his own adventures during his years before the mast, and I would sit at his feet rapt and agog, seeing reincarnations of Morgan, Blackbeard and Long John Silver all mingling in this tanned, salty man. I still think of Nick with pleasure and affection, neither of which is dimmed by the fact that (as I later discovered) the rogue had never in his life seen the sea.

Dan, who looked after the furnaces, would delight my sister and me by letting us watch him shovelling in stacks of coke. The mystery and half-seen glow, red and sinister, beyond the furnace door haunted and impressed me, suggesting the dreaded hell about which I was beginning to learn from the scriptures.

My sister and I were considered very lucky by local children. This was before we went to school where, as I have said, the attitude to our workhouse background was one of resentment. But while we were master and mistress of the highly

15

desirable workhouse gardens, children from the outside world competed for the honour of being invited to play with us.

In one part of the workhouse buildings was what was known as "the blanket room." This was fitted with a ventilator through which you could look directly down on the Boardroom. One Saturday morning my sister and I took a couple of our friends up to this room to let them see the Board of Guardians in session. Constance, being the eldest, warned us to behave ourselves. But at the last minute, I and my high-spirited companions could not resist playing a joke on these very important people. Pulling out two or three wooden shooters, we began pelting the Board of Guardians with split peas. After that we were kept strictly out of the way on those Saturday mornings when the Board met.

One of the Guardians I remember with particular affection, was Miss Bull, owner of a dachshund. She always stopped and had a kind word for me. Yet years later, when the Kaiser's war broke out, the local boys pelted her with stones whenever she was seen with her "filthy little German sausage."

Nowadays there is nothing I like more than to sit down at a well-laid table and eat a properly cooked meal with a knife, fork and spoon. Not so as a child. We loved going off on picnics, usually to Symonds Yat, or some such beauty spot on the river Wye. I would have the task of carrying baskets laden with boiled eggs, lemonade, cakes and jams up the steep slopes. Panting and sweltering I would then help the others to unpack these delicacies, at the same time maintaining a constant fight against predatory wasps and peripatetic ants. It was also my task to stagger down again, carrying the empties. The thought of such an excursion now appals me, but in those blessed days it was heavenly.

There were occasional visits to my father's parents at Lee-on-Solent, then an unspoilt, quiet little seaside resort. I remember taking an instant dislike to a prudish old lady who lived in a house by the sea and who complained bitterly about Naval cadets bathing naked at Spithead, several miles

16

away. She eventually lodged a formal complaint to the Commanding Officer. When he protested that she could not possibly see from where she was, the old dragon replied: "Yes, I can. I have a telescope."

During another holiday, this time at Aldeburgh, I made what perhaps was my first—but by no means last—complaint about the food offered me. I had gone to stay with relations of Maddox, my grandfather's clerk, who, I recollect, paid for our railway tickets in gold. Presumably as a treat for me as well as for themselves, these people had hung up a hare in the pantry and left it there until it stank terribly. Then one mealtime we were given a nauseating red mess. On asking what it was supposed to be, I was told: "Jugged hare." I pushed my plate away, crying: "I am never going to eat this stinking bunny!"

2

THE first dark clouds began to loom over my life at last. What a shock I felt when for the first time I overheard other children referring to our home as "The Spike" or "The Grubber." The way they said it seemed like a personal affront. Our popularity with other children was still strong, thanks to the garden, and the sandpit-cum-rubbish dump, but by living in this serene place I was acquiring what I suppose psychiatrists, with their terrible gift of jargon, would call "an institutional neurosis."

I was, in fact, far happier behind the workhouse walls than beyond them. It gave me great pleasure to wander into my mother's cool larder and watch her dispense dainties to Miss Cork, who would come to collect such items as eggs, lemons, brandy and other delicacies for invalid patients. I remember the clean, crisp swish of starched linen as my mother, the Matron, and Miss Cork, the superintendent nurse, sorted out the goodies while I stood by with watering mouth. I was learning to discriminate between good food and bad, and I had several violent prejudices—long since discarded and, of course, replaced by others. I did not like turkey. I loathed stuffing. I could not bear the sight of plum pudding. So at Christmas time, when all the others were tucking in, I had to content myself with simple fare. To people like my maternal grandfather, this was just another manifestation of pig-headedness. To me it was simply a matter of avoiding food which, to my palate, was poison.

Ours was such a complete world in itself that, whenever I thought of the larger world beyond our walls, it seemed to me a place of limitless cruelty and horror: the inferno beyond the oven door.

Then the worst thing that could possibly have happened to me, took place. My mother recalls how, after I had been up to some mischief or other my father had smiled reassuringly and announced: "Never mind. At present he's your responsibility, but wait till he's old enough to hold a cricket bat. Then I'll tame him."

Unfortunately, he never had his wish. One dreary day in the winter of 1910–11, at the age of thirty, my father died as the result of an appendicitis operation. His last preoccupation was to plan the celebrations at the workhouse for King George V's coronation. Months before the day, he was planning little surprises for the inmates. Everything went off according to plan. My mother saw to that. But the good kindly architect of that day's happiness (so far as our pauper friends were concerned) was in his grave.

Strange how one's memory alights on detail. Through the gloomy memory-patterns of that sad year, I vividly recollect the brightness of that distant Coronation Day. The uniforms of bandsmen, the gay bunting, the Union Jacks drooping in a lazy breeze, the wasp-waisted frilly dresses and the top hats and frock coats of the exalted ladies and gentlemen of the Board of Guardians. The excitement, the feel and sight of warm grass, the cheers and the laughter. Beside me as I write is the Coronation mug given to me, along with the other children. Looking at it I feel a melancholy nostalgia for that gay, portentous childhood day. Yet upon my life, I cannot recall a single detail of that far more important event—my father's passing.

Other pictures loom stronger in the mind. I should explain that, although my mother's appointment as Matron terminated with my father's death, she was reinstated when *her* father was allowed to come back as Master. So her livelihood continued. She had to pay the Board two shillings a week for my sister's and the same for my own board and lodging.

That year I spent many hours alone in the garden. It seemed extraordinarily beautiful. Under the expert eye and hand

19

of the head gardener, Chamberlain, and his assistant, each season brought new wonders and colours to delight me. There was, of course, no lack of extra labour, the inmates being called upon whenever the resident gardeners needed assistance.

On sunny mornings I would look out upon gay herbaceous borders, while all around was a riot of phlox and glorious lilies, of sweet williams, michaelmas daisies or wallflowers. In front of the building were planted the more formal flowers: geraniums, tulips, roses. May trees, lilac, golden rain, and a profusion of laburnums with their bright yellow flowers, wafted their scents across the clean Hereford air. In the greenhouses were masses of lily of the valley and bright red and pink carnations. There was always an abundance of gooseberries, raspberries, loganberries and mulberries for the picking, and wonderfully fresh cucumbers and giant vegetable marrows. I became familiar with the shape and scent of every flowering thing. Sometimes, as I look back at that half-forgotten garden, I long to go off to some such quiet retreat and, forgetting the shams and shallowness of my present life, make what peace I can with God.

Even in that small paradise there were dark corners. One of the inmates was a cranky old woman called Eliza Pritchard, who had an obsession with her bowels. Whenever my mother asked her how she was, the ancient crone would say plaintively: "It's me bowels, mum. I be all stuffed up with bread and meat, mum." One day she wandered into the garden, clasping both hands to her midriff. Those who saw her, assumed that old Eliza was having the usual imaginary trouble with her bowels. She was not seen again for several hours, and then she was found lying under a tree, dead, with her throat cut. That part of the garden became for me a haunted spot.

My other grandfather—my father's father—was a less formidable person than the man who had come back to rule the Workhouse—and incidentally me—with an iron spirit. Unfortunately, I saw very little of my paternal grandfather;

but I remember him telling me: "You seem to be very proud of your memory. When you are as old as I am you will realize how much more important it is to be able to forget." As I face the task of piecing together my scraps and remnants of memory, I begin to understand those words more completely than ever before. For, if I am to be honest, I must return soon to the unhappy relationship between myself and that other grandfather, now once again Master in every sense of our home.

I must recall one Guy Fawkes night when we had an enormous bonfire in the garden around which we cracked fireworks while the guy burned. Just as we were about to light the fire a woman member of the Board of Guardians arrived to watch the fun. For some reason my sister and I had rigged the guy out in women's clothing, complete with blouse, skirt, an old pair of elastic-sided boots, and a toque —the hat much favoured by the ladies of that era. Patting me benevolently on the head, this grand visitor said: "I see you have made yourself a lady guy. Now whoever can she be?"

"Mrs. Pankhurst," I said, innocently naming the suffragist at that time much in the news.

The lady turned very pale. "I do not think this is at all amusing," she said to my mother and stalked away. We later learnt that our visitor was herself an ardent suffragette. Through the Board my grandfather was officially notified of my irreverence and, of course, the old man made things extremely hot for us.

That year my sister and I began to attend school. I was five years old, and used to be taken by one of the inmates to Miss Ford's school in Grenfell Road. Here we were taught to write on slates and add and subtract figures. I liked Miss Ford and I also enjoyed learning. It therefore took no great effort to teach me, so long as I was interested in a subject. For a special treat, if we were very good, we would be given a wonderful soft chalk which did not scratch when drawn

21

across the slate. I loved handling that soft chalk—it was bliss.

Close to the school was an inn, the Rose and Crown on the Ledbury road. Sometimes I would find myself staring at this quite ordinary pub and making it the object of all sorts of romantic conjectures: creaking inn signs, highwaymen galloping along the highway, men in three-cornered hats raising tankards and toasting Bonnie Prince Charlie. In those days, inns seemed romantic places. *Eheu! fugaces labuntur anni.* Only the other day, a woman who is now a Mrs. Smith wrote to remind me that she was the former Mary Chave whose father kept the Rose and Crown, and that she was a big girl about to leave the school when my sister and I arrived.

I loved most of all the moment when I would be met from school, either by my mother or one of my aunts, Ethel or Edith. Although my sister was supposed to be in charge of me, Mother knew how much I relied on seeing her and met me whenever she could manage it. Though I had only been away from her since two o'clock (an inmate fetched us back to the workhouse for dinner) it was always reassuring to see her after school.

Whenever we were left to come home by ourselves there was usually trouble of some sort or other. On one occasion my sister and I pulled a cap off a little boy in the lane at the back of the workhouse and we were rebuked by an elderly lady, the wife of a local prebendary, who said: "I will speak to your mother." I was upset because I did not want Mother to be bothered, since all our little misdemeanours were grossly magnified by our ever-vigilant grandfather.

Sister Constance and I also found great pleasure, when left to ourselves, in popping our heads suddenly over the workhouse walls and shouting at people going by. This sometimes drew groups of angry urchins round the walls, and their shouts of "Spike" and "Grubber" led to further complaints.

After three years at Miss Ford's I was able to go to the local "Blue" School, an old arrangement by which you paid sixpence a week to get a slightly better education than that of the ordinary elementary schools. This ancient Bluecoat foundation, situated in Blue School Street, Hereford, was an offspring of Christ's Hospital, but by no means as illustrious as the parent institution.

My master there was a man called "Billy" Caldwell, a fiery, dapper little man with a sharp, upended waxed moustache. This galvanic despot—he used to dance rather than walk—was a great disciplinarian who terrified us boys. The idea that any of us should be late was unforgivable. It was as a result of my being two minutes behind time one morning that I first experienced the cane on the hand, which I always thought was an unsatisfactory method of punishment. As I became more practised, I used to get a certain amount of fun from pulling the hand back as the cane was coming down. This sometimes had an unsettling effect on the excitable "Billy" and his second swipe would not be half so vicious.

One of the women teachers who made a considerable impression on me at that time was a Miss Groom: but I was chastened to find, when I met her a few years ago, that she has no recollection of having known me as a schoolboy. I would have liked to feel I made some impression on my elders!

I respected "Billy" Caldwell, but was glad to see the back of him when I was elected to the Royal Orphanage, Wolverhampton. In her determination to have me properly educated, Mother had been hard put to finding a suitably good but inexpensive school. By this time my nuisance value to my grandfather was wearing us all out. Although Mother knew I had no great wish to leave her side, it was considered wiser to impose some form of outside discipline on me.

What to do with me? My father's numerous family were quite unhelpful. Just then there occurred a small incident which I am sure was the last straw as far as my grandfather was concerned. Sandford, the under gardener, with whom I always associated delicious tomatoes, was inordinately proud of his vast vegetable plot. One day I was loafing about his cottage, watching his wife cooking. Her great speciality was making "White Puddings", which consisted of fat from a recently killed pig, bound together by groats and milk. On being given a mouthful of this—none that I have tasted since was quite so good—I went off and collected my big red wooden engine.

Off I went across the garden, trailing my engine on a piece of string. In my fancy I was making a splendid circular tour of all the wild, romantic places about which I was then reading: the American pine forests of Fenimore Cooper, the highlands and islands of Robert Louis Stevenson, the dark green hills and castle-studded rivers of the brothers Grimm. Blithely I dragged my cumbersome engine all through what I thought were weeds. They were actually vetches, Sandford's pride. The gardener dashed off in a giant rage to my grandfather, and that was the beginning of the end of my carefree days at the Union Workhouse, Hereford.

3

In order to get me into Wolverhampton's Royal Orphanage, Mother had to write round to all the Patrons and subscribers of the School which then, as still today, is "entirely supported by voluntary contributions." It was founded in 1850 when it was known as the Wolverhampton Orphan Asylum. In the 1920s it was recognized by the Board of Education as a Secondary School; and King George VI gave his permission for the new name of the Royal Wolverhampton School in the Centenary Year of 1950. Founded to provide shelter and education for children orphaned in the cholera epidemic in 1848, by 1916, when I arrived there, it was housed in an imposing building off Penn Road, Wolverhampton, and it harboured 220 boys and 130 girls.

Before I went there, however, Mother twice was obliged to circularize my "canvassing card," containing my photograph and details of our circumstances. I was delighted when Mother's first attempt was unsuccessful. We had gone to tea at the home of a local dentist whose son, Freddy Volpé, a lad about two years older than myself, took me aside and warned me not to let myself be sent there. With great skill and vivid description he drew hideous pictures of what went on there and told me that I should hate the school as much as he did.

Then one dreadful afternoon my mother told me that I had "got in." I wept. I went to my room and cried myself to sleep. When, a few weeks later, I did have to leave home, I did so with tears and lamentation.

It was on August 28, 1916, that my mother took me in a smelly old horse-drawn cab from the Low Level Station to the Royal Orphanage. I have written elsewhere of how we arrived carrying a suitcase in which Mother was to take back the clothes I was wearing. What is beyond my power of description is the dreadful feeling of finality, the terrifying and almost unbelievable sense of leaving behind for ever the carefree days.

I was a very spoilt little boy, badly behaved, selfish and liable to violent fits of temper if I did not get my own way quickly enough. Now all I knew was that I was going to be separated from my mother, who had been my protector and shield, and that I was going to be locked up and thrust into a uniform which I thought was very silly, anyhow.

The newcomers were "received" and examined by a Dr. Dent whom I liked at once, but under the eagle eye of the Matron, whom I felt I should never like. Then we were given our uniforms and I was horrified by the shirt and terrible broadcloth pants, and *boots*! Grotesquely clad, we were taken back to say goodbye. My mother was upset by the sight of me, but she was able to smile and tell me she had seen the dinner and that it "looked very nice."

Some time later we new boys were taken to a room where, to my unspeakable shame, we all had to get into a big bath together under the supervision of a maid. This was the final humiliation. I could not remember when any woman except my mother had seen me naked. I cried myself to sleep and awoke to stark reality. I had come to school. I was "in," and the first thing I did was to copy a boy's calendar on which I was to tick off the long weary days to Visiting Day, and then to Christmas.

We were rigidly segregated. The passing of notes between girls and boys was unthinkable. Even the exchange of glances in chapel was frowned upon. Our life was highly institutional. There were only two terms a year with a month's holiday at Christmas and six weeks in the summer. Whitsuntide and Easter week holidays were spent at school. There was one Visiting Day in the middle of each term.

Boys always wore the dreadful heavy boots which so

26

depressed me on seeing them for the first time. We also wore brown stockings, moleskin breeches, long blue coats and white bibs—just like Christ's Hospital but not so smart. Girls wore hideous blue tunics, stiff white collars and cuffs and unbelievably hideous flat straw hats. The food was adequate, but quite disgusting.

Routine soon established its drably rigid pattern. We got up in the unheated dormitories at six-thirty, lined up to go downstairs for a strip-wash in cold water (hot water was unheard of, except for the weekly bath) and then into school at seven-fifteen for three-quarters of an hour of "prep" before breakfast.

There was never any doubt what breakfast would be. Sunday, Monday, Wednesday and Friday: bread and margarine, and occasionally jam or marmalade, with cocoa. Tuesday, Thursday and Saturday: porridge as well. Two bits of bread when there was porridge, four when there was not. And this delicious food was eaten off chipped enamel plates, the cocoa drunk from chipped enamel mugs. When our relations sent us eggs we were allowed to put our names on them and have them cooked for us.

School began at nine and went on till twelve-fifteen. Then came dinner. There was never any doubt about that, either! Sunday: Bully beef and beetroot with potatoes boiled in their skins (they were always boiled in their skins!), followed by stewed prunes. Monday: Mince, followed by rice pudding. Tuesday: Bully beef followed by "gobby," a kind of fruit pudding in which we found the oddest things from rats' tails and bits of string to fragments of sacking. Wednesday: Fish (boiled cod) and potatoes; rice pudding. Thursday's dinner I have forgotten but I know it was something awful—probably "Stew." Friday: a different kind of "gobby"—a kind of meat pudding which consisted of a soggy crust and a lump of rainbow-coloured fat. No one ever ate all the lumps of fat.

One day, shortly after I arrived, the Headmaster complained about waste. Now it was an understood thing that

27

the bread plate was used for unwanted bits of fat, the plate being passed from boy to boy as and when he needed it. That day the Head chose to follow up his words by making a tour of the dining hall. Unfortunately, he saw this plate stacked with chewed fat which happened at that moment to be in front of me. He did not ask if it were mine. He simply ordered me to eat it up.

I looked at the messy pile with a nasty feeling beginning to churn up inside.

"Eat it up, boy!" the Head roared. "We do not want any waste here."

"But, sir, I didn't put any of that stuff on the plate," I said.

"Eat it up," the Head said, pushing my face towards the mess. So I had no alternative but to swallow the other boys' leavings, and promptly be sick on the spot.

Our routine continued with afternoon school between two and four o'clock, except on Wednesdays and Saturdays. Tea was at six and always exactly the same as breakfast except for the porridge. No more was eaten between then and bedtime except one dry biscuit, which was handed to us at eight-thirty. Wednesday and Saturday afternoons would be devoted to "games." There was an asphalt yard and a playroom and a covered playground. I didn't enjoy games very much, though later I did get round to running and once won the junior 220 yards, the prize for which was a small box camera.

We were always bathed in batches of twenty at a time in a great tub. After my initial humiliation and shock, I got accustomed to this but I never became reconciled to the state of the water which was not changed for each batch. If you were in the third batch you had to push back a sea of scum as you went in.

We were astonishingly well taught. Indeed, there was little else to do except learn. The headmaster was one of the most remarkable men I have ever known. He was the Rev. Frank Lampitt, known as "Dad." Feared and hated by most

Constance and G.H.

"A proud little chanticleer."

"Always years older in common sense."

"Father was universally esteemed"

of the boys, he loomed over our lives, a grim figure with a grey moustache stained by tobacco chewing and incessant smoking. When he spoke, tobacco juice would spray all over us.

I now realize what he was up against. His own salary was meagre. Not a single man on the staff had a degree. We were, remember, in the middle of the First World War and the maximum salary paid to the assistant masters was £70 a year. The only good masters were very young "old boys" waiting for military call-up. Others came from the hedges by the look of them. Some drank, others were illiterate. But a few of them were able and efficient.

"Dad" Lampitt therefore took it upon himself—since he could get no master capable of doing it—to keep order unaided. He imposed what was virtually a reign of terror. He came round the dormitories to keep order as we got up and dressed. Then he would preside over breakfast in the dining hall. Between rising and breakfast time he gave extra tuition in the big schoolroom to advanced scholars, then taught for every period, morning and afternoon. He would take his seat in the hall at dinner time and go on to teach all the afternoon; and then again during evening "prep." Finally he would supervise the masters' rounds of the dormitories. He was already a very tired man when I arrived at the school in 1916.

We did not have evening chapel in those days. Lampitt would conduct a service early in the afternoon, and instead of evening services he would read aloud to us from such books as *Dombey and Son*. Whenever anyone's attention began to wander, he would look up from his massive volume and roar at the culprit: "Come out, you! You seem to forget that my spectacles reflect everything!"

I never did anything so exciting as to run away from school, though I often thought about it. The fate of those who tried was so awful that I always stayed put. Shortly before evening "prep," some time during my first year at Wolverhampton, we were all ordered to assemble in a classroom. We filed in, wondering what catastrophe lay ahead. At last "Dad" Lampitt stalked in, followed by two boys who had tried to run away. I think their names were Mayrick and Otty.

One after the other, the boys were soundly flogged until I was almost sick with shock and nausea. This dreadful spectacle checked me whenever my thoughts strayed toward the freedom of the outside world.

While I was never actually hungry, I was always ravenous for titbits: chocolate creams, buns, ginger pop. Mother used to send me pocket money to buy little extras, but one day Lampitt stopped that, telling her: "He must accept only what is given to him at the school. The boy already has a tendency to show off."

So I wrote to Mother telling her that I had broken a window and needed five shillings to pay for its repair. This I duly received in the post. But when I wrote and told her that I had lost a textbook and needed to replace it, Mother had just planned to visit me at school and arrived to take me out to tea. Not having been informed that she was coming, I was scared when I was sent for to put my best coat on and report to the headmaster's study. I was relieved and overjoyed to find Mother there, holding a promising looking suitcase.

"Your mother has come to take you to tea," Lampitt said.

As we were about to leave, to my horror Mother produced five separate shillings which she handed to the Head, saying: "Here is the money for the textbook Gilbert lost."

Lampitt said nothing.

That night, before he began one of his readings from Dickens, he said: "Stand up, Harding, liar and thief! I keep my money in my study in a cash box in the lower left hand drawer. The box is never locked. If you ever want money, you now know where to steal it—from me, not your mother."

Lampitt then flung the five shillings at me, ordering me to pick them up. I refused.

"Pick it up!" he shouted.

I slunk from my desk and, on all fours, groped for the money.

"Now get out!" Lampitt thundered, when I had collected my pieces of silver. I did so, feeling as Judas Iscariot must have done before he strung himself to the *Cercis siliquastrum*.

I was unable to conform altogether. For one thing, I refused to be guided. When Ramsay MacDonald visited Wolverhampton during an election tour, we were forbidden to go into the town. Naturally, I went. I was not a particular admirer or supporter of Mr. MacDonald, but I resented being told what to do. There is still in the files of the Wolverhampton *Express and Star* a picture of my shaking hands with MacDonald as he left the Star and Garter Hotel.

Although this happened somewhat late in my school career, I was busily laying the foundations of unorthodoxy from the start. Sometimes it was merely a routine brush with authority. I was once given a hundred lines for talking in class. I was furious. And as I laboriously wrote out the banal words *I must not talk in class: I must not talk in class:* my anger against the obviously inept, manifestly illiterate apprentice teacher who had inflicted this punishment mounted till I felt an insane impulse somehow to injure him. The moment I had written my last line I went off to this master's bedroom. Finding nobody about I began to make him an apple-pie bed. Unfortunately, another master chose that moment to pay the absent master a call. He caught me as I was about to push an alarum clock into the mangled bedclothes. I received eight of the best with no intervening protection.

One of the masters who drank, was so far gone as an alcoholic that we were fairly safe in ragging him. We used to keep our trunks or boxes under the bed. Whenever it was this unfortunate man's turn to do the nightly rounds we placed our boxes at the foot of our beds. There was always the risk that Lampitt might be on the prowl and ask what the box was doing in that position, but the risk was worth it.

Whenever the pickled master walked in—moving unsteadily and holding the ends of the beds to keep himself from toppling —he would inevitably trip over one of the boxes and come down with a crash. Too fuddled to notice what was happening, he would still be collecting what was left of his wits while one of us nipped out of bed and pushed the box back into its place. Then we would all sit up and complain loudly that he had woken us up. "Whisky Bob," as we called him, did not stay long at the school.

Another cause of nocturnal disturbance were the Zeppelin raids over West Bromwich. I must confess that, timid as I then was about so many things, the moment the Zepps approached the sky above the school, I used to sit up in bed tingling with excitement that was not at all unpleasurable. I have since been told by medical men that this is a common occurrence during moments of threatened danger, and I sometimes experienced the same reaction years later in the Second World War.

One thing, oddly enough, did not upset our slumbers. The school was near the Sunbeam Motor works. All through the war years there was a constant roar of engines being tested. When the war stopped and night shifts were called off, the noise also ceased. For many weeks we found we could not sleep. Our ears missed the noise.

Whenever I got into mischief it was usually my lot to be caught out. After an outbreak of playing with mirrors in the sun, when we menaced everybody by suddenly casting blinding reflections into unsuspecting eyes, we were forbidden to carry mirrors at all. I did not hand mine in. One sunny afternoon, during a French class under a master who was very good at French but no good at discipline, I was having a glorious time with my mirror when, looking into it I saw the reflection of "Dad" Lampitt's outraged face. The inevitable beating followed.

Lampitt's method of teaching us would make modern educationists shudder. We learnt everything by rote, parrot fashion. We were terrified of him as he stalked into the room. He was, I suppose, a brutal man, but his methods worked. Out of sixteen candidates who entered for the Cambridge Preliminary during any of his teaching years, sixteen would pass.

The much beloved English master was Louis Frederick Stiles, known as "Stilly." His methods were effectively simple. For instance, he would take a play by Shakespeare, a collection of poetry, and a prose book, and extract certain passages. These he would set us to learn.

Then he would invite one of us to his room. This was always a treat in itself for we would always go just before breakfast time and, when that time came, we would be offered a cup of coffee, and a bit of bacon and a slice of bread soaked in bacon fat. We would then be asked to recite any one of the passages he had set us, and he would interrupt us sometimes to say "No, no no! It's written as music. Sing it. Let your voice *sing*." If at the end of the session you heard him say: "Thank you, lad, I enjoyed that," you went off in high spirits. Moreover, you had committed to mind a few more of the noblest passages of literature, to remember all your life.

On "Dad's" birthday we boys would be dunned by the monitors for a subscription towards a present. We could pay anything between a penny and threepence—but it paid to be generous. On the morning of his birthday the Senior Monitors would go to his room before breakfast and say: "The boys would like to see you, sir."

"Dad" pretended to be surprised. Then, on his being led in, one of us would read from an illuminated address. It always began exactly the same. "The Rev. F. Lampitt, B.A." we would hear. "Sir, on this your birthday, we, the boys . . ." Finally we got round to giving him his present; usually something connected with smoking—a new pipe, a pipe rack, a tobacco case, cigars.

The pantomime would end with "Dad" producing a bag filled with pennies. This he would pass over to a monitor who, with subscription list in hand, then doled out exactly double the subscription tendered: twopence to those who had contributed a penny, fourpence to those who had given twopence, and sixpence to those who had parted with threepence. Then Lampitt would say: "Well, birthdays should be happy occasions, so after breakfast you may have a day free from your studies." This amiable ritual would end with three rousing cheers for the Head—and for a week there would be no more beatings.

Towards the end of his tired life, "Dad" was a very sick man indeed. Not that we boys suspected it. Wartime strain killed him. Yet he went on teaching us till the end, going through the lessons with crystal lucidity. One morning he was explaining a geometrical theorem, painstakingly writing down the various riders on the blackboard. Before wiping them out he asked, as he usually did: "Any questions? Any doubts?" Our silence signified that we thoroughly understood what he had been telling us. The next day he returned to the subject.

"Harding," he suddenly said, "come out."

I went up to his platform.

"Do the eleventh rider."

I was completely stumped.

"I'm afraid I can't remember it, sir," I confessed.

"You agree," Lampitt said quietly, "that yesterday I asked this class, 'Any questions? Any doubts?' "

"Yes, sir."

"And that there was no reply?"

"Yes, sir."

"Did you not understand what I was telling you?"

"Not quite, sir."

"Then you were lying yesterday?"

"Yes, sir."

Lampitt looked helplessly at me and then turned away with an irritated shrug.

"I shall leave this room before I lose my temper," he said

curtly, and went out. We sat at our desks for a long time before we realized that he was not coming back. That afternoon we learnt he had been taken ill. Within a week he was dead. I think that none of us knew what a friend he had lost.

4

LAMPITT was at heart—as I now know—an Anglo-Catholic. It was not until we senior boys filed into his room to see him "laid out" that we noticed he was dressed in strange clerical clothing. Looking down into the coffin we found that he wore a chasuble, stole, and alb. I was oddly fascinated by this early glimpse of Catholic drama—a fascination which was to obsess me more and more as I grew older. I have since tried, with no result, to have a memorial erected to "Dad" though I believe that there is now a Bible or a reading desk in the Chapel.

Lampitt was succeeded by a young, handsome, enlightened and indulgent clergyman. This was the Rev. William Louis Allen, who came to us from the King's School, Chester, manifestly determined to improve matters. He immediately created a sensation by taking for the text of his first sermon the passage from St. John, "I am come that they might have life, and that they might have it more abundantly."

It was a mistake, so far as I was concerned. Lampitt, more than any other man before or since, understood that strain in me which will not be coerced. No matter how much I like, or even try to respect anyone, I have a quick flair for knowing exactly when someone is trying to sell me something. Sometimes I let the farce go on for a while, but it is my misfortune (perhaps) to detect the "phony" in a person frequently before that person does himself. So it was with Allen. A splendid man, with fine ideals and excellent ideas, I found that he was trying to sell himself just a trifle too glibly. I liked him though: he had great charm.

Lampitt, for all his brutality, was an exceptionally honest man. The new headmaster, meticulously honest about most things, was deluding himself as well. I know there can be few Albert Schweitzers in this world, but that does not prevent my social antennae from discovering the false notes the moment they are struck. This applies equally to myself; and that perhaps is the one good reason why I shall never be a completely happy man.

I watched with amusement the missionary activities of Lampitt's successor. More human and humane than "Dad," Allen introduced many much-needed reforms. He started singing classes, amateur theatricals, and, though not for a long while and not without a struggle, got rid of some of the more rigid rules of segregation between the girls' and boys' schools.

In later years I learnt to abhor and detest social and racial segregation as much as any other aspect of human deficiency. I am sure it would have been a good thing if we had been allowed to see more of the girls; I might even have learnt the art of living permanently beside a woman without each of us driving the other to frenzies of exasperation and misery. It was a great advance, I remember, when the girls were eventually allowed to come to our debates.

On the whole, we youngsters thankfully welcomed Allen's new régime of enlightenment. What we did not realize was that the younger man had far more time in which to carry out his plans. The war being over he was able to get a better staff and better facilities. In many ways he had far less responsibility than the worn-out, overworked and harassed Lampitt ever had. Being a "new broom," Allen was able to persuade the governors to pay better salaries to his new team of teachers. Not long after his arrival the Board of Education recognized the school as a secondary school, and all was set for a progressive future.

In particular I welcomed the introduction of full-scale theatrical classes. I was, as it turned out, quite a good actor. Among the parts I played at that time were Shylock, King Richard II, and Prince Hal in *Henry IV*, Part I. I had a great compliment paid to the authenticity of my performance while acting Richard II. Junior boys were allowed to come and see the dress rehearsal at which only the principals were fully made up. In the play I was killed by Sir Pierce of Exton, played by a boy called Bird who, without his black beard, looked just like Bird.

After I had been stabbed and was sinking prostrate to the floor of my dungeon, I had to say the lines:

> "*Mount, mount, my soul! thy seat is up on high;*
> *Whilst my gross flesh sinks downward, here to die.*"

So effective, apparently, was my delivery of this spicy piece of "ham" that a little boy in the front row exclaimed in horror: "Gosh! Isn't Bird a sneak!"

When, also in this play, I had to kiss the queen goodbye, I regret to say that I came, quite literally, unstuck. The queen was played in strict Elizabethan fashion, by a good-looking boy called Stanley Lester. After the moving couplet,

> "*One kiss shall stop our mouths, and dumbly part;*
> *Thus give I mine, and thus take I thy heart,*"

I had to go forward and plant a last, long kiss on Lester's lips. This always made us laugh, but our master, stressing that Shakespeare had clearly ordered that the kiss be given on the mouth, insisted that we stopped behaving like silly little asses and did the thing thoroughly. So we did; with the result that, during an actual performance before a crowded house, I found my false beard firmly stuck to Lester's face. When, at last, I managed to wrench myself away, I left more than half of my kingly moustache under the queen's nose.

This regal incident reminds me of the first of my four encounters, to date, with members of our Royal family. This was the visit to the school of King George VI, then Duke of York. There was great excitement long before the day, an extra dash of drama having been added by the warning note sent to the school by a suspected assassin. About this time two I.R.A. men had murdered Field-Marshal Sir Henry Wilson in Eaton Square. One of these men was called Reg Dunn. The effect can easily be imagined when we boys learnt that the Secretary had received a note from some crackbrained unfortunate warning him: "YOU HAD BETTER LOOK OUT. A PAL OF REG DUNN."

Frantic security measures were put into effect. I think the police made the school build a bridge across the road between the forecourt where the Duke was due to step from his car, and the playing field where an extra large marquee was erected to shelter him from the weather and now, presumably, an assassin's bullet.

However, no pal of Reg Dunn materialized. His Royal Highness seemed more apprehensive about the rows of staring boys and girls than of any assassin. I remember feeling quite sorry for him as he stood on a beflagged platform, gamely disguising his extreme nervousness with a determined show of cheerfulness. I had done pretty well that year, it seems, and eventually I found myself going up to the platform to receive a prize for the third time. Twice the Duke contented himself with a kindly smile as he handed me the prize. This time I suddenly realized that he was about to make some remark. For what seemed an eternity I waited for the Duke to speak. I became apprehensive, wondering, as the seconds ticked by, if I had forgotten to brush my hair properly or knot my tie neatly.

At last, the words came. "What," said the Duke slowly, "you—again?"

"Yes, sir," I replied, and bowed my way off the platform, feeling like an Elizabethan courtier whose monarch has just decided not to have his head chopped off in the Tower, after all.

My last two years at school were largely devoted to loafing. Lessons no longer worried me. All you needed was a good memory and good teachers, and I had both. I was able to spend a little more time beyond the school walls and cultivate outside friends. There was, I remember, a man called Alfred Van Damm who conducted the orchestra of the Queen's

Cinema, Wolverhampton. He would let some of us older fellows into the cinema show for nothing and give us tea for nothing. Many of us had good reason to be grateful to him for a good tea and an hour or two of pleasant conversation. It made a change.

Then I would explore the countryside. A favourite trip was to Sedgley Beacon, built at the time of the Armada, where I would turn my back on cricket or soccer (both of which I avoided like the plague) and relax with a good book, or merely laze and ponder upon the infinite mystery of living.

Allen let me do as I liked. I got on very well with him. Too well, perhaps, so far as my acquiring any real discipline was concerned. I stopped being in any particular form and was helping to teach the little boys in Form 2B. Sometimes, when the French master was away, I also instructed the elder boys in Form 4B in that language.

Yet there was one crucial obstacle between me and the next step towards a Cambridge scholarship. I found examinations frightening. I disliked the feeling that people were prying into your mind simply to find out what you did *not* know. So when three of us sat for the Fowler Scholarship, worth £250 a year, another boy called Philip Chavasse won it. He was a fine mathematician and his examination nerves were better than mine.

Chavasse won the Scholarship and went to Clare College. The idea was that I should go to one of the "redbrick" provincial universities. Having set myself on the idea of going to Cambridge, I was bitterly upset by my failure. Then just as I was preparing for the following year's examinations I had wonderful news. Chavasse wanted to leave Cambridge, so the scholarship was given to me, after all. The rest of my schooldays were spent in complete idleness as I waited blithely to take my place among the young gentlemen of the university.

5

On October 25, 1925, I went up to Queens' College, Cambridge, to read Modern Languages—French and German. If my stern but revered headmaster at the Royal Orphanage, Wolverhampton, the Rev. Frank Lampitt, had not died when he did, I think I would have got an open scholarship. This would have netted me between £60 and £80 more than the £250 Fowler Scholarship upon which I was sustained yearly during my stay at the University—in retrospect, the happiest three years of my life. Lampitt's death, some two-thirds of the way through my school days, had removed a powerful incentive to work.

I wish I could write lyrically of first breathless moments at Cambridge, but I had already been twice up as an unsuccessful candidate for an open scholarship, and the journey from the hideous railway station, past the ghastly war memorial and uninspired Victorian business premises, to my college merely reminded me of the disappointed enthusiasms of those earlier visits.

My arrival, therefore, on a bleak autumn day was, in every sense of the word, an anti-climax. I was mainly concerned with wondering what to say if people asked me why I was not wearing an old school tie. In those days, my school did not possess one. Even now it is pleasant to remember the relief I felt when, after a week or two, it became clear that nobody cared sufficiently about my lack of a tie to make any comment at all. I was, nevertheless, always a little envious of anyone who possessed splendid old school ties and blazers.

My first lodgings were in Derby Street. My landlady had a wooden leg with which, it was rumoured, she beat her husband. I did not find my quarters there at all congenial and I was glad to move, after a while, to Mrs. Gray's comfortable home at the edge of Grantchester Meadows. It has always been my way to form immediate likes and dislikes. My second Cambridge landlady and I took to each other on sight, and we have remained friends ever since.

As a freshman, one's first obligation was to see the Senior Tutor. Mine was a highly nervous physicist called Sleeman, who would first make a point of saying "No" to every request we made and then talk himself into saying "Yes." Soon after I went up I particularly wanted to see a new Coward play. When I called on Sleeman and asked for an exeat, the interview proceeded on the following lines.

"Why do you want an exeat, Harding?"

"To go up to London, sir."

"What for?"

"To see a play, sir."

"A *play*?" Sleeman's face registered infinite pain. "What sort of play, pray."

"The new piece by Noël Coward, sir."

"Certainly not."

"But, sir——"

"Not another word. You have come here to work, Harding, not to go gadding off to the London playhouses."

Then after a long silence, Sleeman continued: "Have you read the critical notices of this play?"

"Quite a number of them, sir."

"What did you think of them?"

"Very encouraging, sir. They have made me extremely curious to see the actual play."

"Mm, yes. I agree with you there. That fellow Agate's comments were very much to the point, I thought."

"Very."

"They interested me."

"Yes, sir."

"Very well, my boy. You may have the exeat. But be sure to work hard on your return."

"Yes, sir. Thank you, sir."

42

"Oh, and let me know if the play came up to your expectations."

Sleeman was a lovable man, somewhat afraid of undergraduates. Indeed I always expected him to dive for cover under his desk whenever I entered his sanctum. Somehow he managed to survive the many ordeals of seeing me, and invariably I got my own way.

Yet, for all his timidity, he had a hard, basic core of pluck. A brittle dreamer, his eyes were fixed on the distant mountain tops. He could hardly wait for the end of term, when he would set off for the Alps and forget all about us in the great solitudes.

The President of our college was Dr. Fitzpatrick, another somewhat nervous and retiring man. He lived quietly, seeming to emerge but seldom from his comfortable President's lodging, with its long timbered gallery built in the reign of Edward IV. Despite his retiring nature, he conscientiously applied himself to knowing each undergraduate individually. He liked everyone to call upon him at least once a term, the time fixed for these visits being usually after "hall" on Sunday evenings. Apart from these semi-formal visits, you could not go down at the end of term without paying a further call on the President, who had to sign the exeat, and if you had failed to make a Sunday evening call during the past term he wanted to know why.

It was amusing to go and see him. He had hardly any conversation, and his wife was also painfully nervous. It was a current joke that the one subject they would always discuss was the new bridge built over Coe Fen. I fear I never helped him toward this absorbing topic, but counted the minutes while the old gentleman made frantic, inarticulate sounds before asking in an agonized voice: "By the way, Harding, what do you think of the new bridge over Coe Fen?"

The President was a Christ's man. He had been elected by the fellows to be President of Queens' because the college, which was a poor one, always looked for a man with private

43

means to be its head. They did very well out of Fitzpatrick, who restored the gallery as well as the old court to its original medieval splendour. Queens' being one of the poorer colleges, care was taken by the dons to keep down the cost of living. For what I think was £36 a term we were provided with dinner in hall. At other colleges "hall" was compulsory only twice a week. We at Queens' were not encouraged to "sign off" simply by being made to pay for our meals in the hall whether we were there or not. We poorer scholars were deeply indebted to the wonderful Mr. Chamberlain, our college Kitchen Steward who has only just retired after nearly fifty years of service. Thanks to his care and foresight our food was easily the best in the university.

Our £36 included dues, tuition, coal and "commons"—a good sized pat of butter a week and a loaf of bread and some milk every day. If we incurred a bill at the college buttery of more than £10, we had to see the tutor before getting his consent for more credit—and if he knew one was poor one simply did not get it.

Somehow, even in those comparatively prosperous days, my money never seemed adequate. My mother began by having the scholarship money paid to her direct, and from this she made me an allowance. But I soon persuaded her to let me have the money paid into my newly-formed bank account, since when, I fear, I have never been financially stable. At Cambridge, once I possessed a cheque book, I found it all too easy to obtain anything I wanted without paying for it. Local tailors, shirtmakers, grocers, wine merchants and tobacconists were only too glad to let the gentlemen of the university have unlimited credit.

Queens', aware of the danger of this, compelled tradesmen to send bills to the college of all undergraduates who owed more than £5 at the end of any term. It was the custom for freshmen to live out the first two years, coming into college only for the last year. Although I lived modestly, and while my debts never got really out of hand, whenever I look back on those three happy years I feel that I really know the true meaning of the worn-out phrase, "halcyon days."

My French supervisor, Mr. Momber, and my German supervisor, Mr. Bennett, soon gave up trying to make me work diligently at these subjects. So I abandoned them for History, a notoriously easy subject, and settled down to enjoying myself.

To my surprise, I found myself easily making friends. I began to frequent the debates at the Union Society and joined several clubs. I also made it my eccentric target to know the dean of every college and dine at each one of Cambridge's seventeen college halls at least once before I went down. I succeeded in reaching this target, but not without occasional difficulties.

It was not long before I found myself speaking on every kind of subject at the Union. While I like to think now that I might have been President, I never stood for that reason all-too-typical of me—that I have always had a fear of being shown up. Even today, I rarely undertake to do a thing unless I am certain that I can put on a reasonably good show. I was, however, thrice elected to the Committee, of which I am now a permanent member.

6

WHENEVER I try to remember what I liked most about Cambridge, I find myself desperately trying to fight through the conventional images; yet precious memories persist. Punts and gramophones on the river; bathing at Byron's Pool or loafing and sunbathing at the university bathing sheds; breakfast with other people, either in their rooms or mine; interminable talks; sherry parties; midnight gatherings—how happy one could be in those days on three or four bottles of beer!

During my long sojourn at Cambridge my only real athletic venture occurred shortly before my second Christmas there. At the end of term, five of us decided to save money on railway fares by walking the fifty miles to London, where we intended to spend the holiday.

The hospitable walls of Cambridge were fading in a grey December dusk when we struck out along the main London road. We continued to walk throughout a bright, beautiful, moonlit night. Not far from Colney Hatch—which I felt ought to have been our proper target—I almost collapsed. However, some time after a cold dawn, we reached the top of Highgate Hill and saw the domes and spires and gasometers of the capital. As we dispersed to our various destinations, my feet dragging heavily over the hard, hard pavements, I fervently echoed Henry Ford's wise maxim: "Exercise is bunk. If you are healthy you don't need it; if you are sick you shouldn't take it." Arriving at my host's house in Ashley Gardens, Westminster, I pitched through the front door and just managed to crawl up to bed, where I remained for the next two days.

I think the Union was the activity which gave me the most pleasure. Many of the presidents during my time at Cambridge have since become distinguished. David Hardman, who became Parliamentary Secretary to the Ministry of Education, was an outstanding debater, even then. So was Patrick Devlin, now a High Court Judge. Michael Ramsey, now Bishop of Durham, and Hugh ("Mac") Foot, now Her Majesty's Governor and Captain General in and over the Colony of Jamaica, were also marked out for high distinction early in life. We also enjoyed the early wit and brilliant dialectics of Geoffrey Crowther, now editor of *The Economist*.

We had distinguished visiting speakers. The one who impressed me most was the Earl of Birkenhead. He came to defend the Baldwin Government, speaking on the time-honoured motion "that this House has no confidence in His Majesty's Government." It was a wonderful speech.

The distinguished lawyer-wit had had a good deal to drink. Towards the end of his discourse he said: "Now Sir, we come to the great strike." A very left-wing undergraduate of unfortunate appearance, with wild red hair, thick glasses and a face disfigured with septic acne, was sitting beside me in a state of obvious agitation. The reference to the strike was too much for the whispy firebrand, who called out with a Cockney accent: "Stroik? You mean lock-out!"

Birkenhead turned towards our part of the house, a terrible expression of scorn on his suffused and handsome face. "Good God," thundered he, "am I in the Cambridge Union Society or in some festering slum of Wapping? Is it conceivable that any creature, however base, sordid and forlorn, who has been brought even into momentary contact with such a seat of learning as this place pretends to be," ("F.E." was an Oxford man) "can describe this unparalleled affront to the Imperial Crown and dignity of this realm as a lock-out? Will my interrupter stand up?"

"I certainly will," said my unhappy neighbour.

Birkenhead's features seemed to summon even more impressive lines of contempt and horror.

"Sit down, sir," he hissed. "Sit down. Your distressing

appearance is more than an adequate commentary on your untimely interruption."

I am glad to say that the unfortunate interrupter joined in the general laughter.

After the debate we adjourned to the Committee Room to drink whisky and soda and eat sandwiches. Knowing a thing or two by this time about Birkenhead, I saw that there was brandy for him. "Splendid perception," said he to me. "You deserve to go far in life." On such wayward threads hangs the balance of personality; for I was now completely won over by this monumentally arrogant man.

On another occasion, I debated with Sir Arthur Conan Doyle. The subject, I need hardly say, was Spiritualism. I happened to question the sense of women in psychic spasms giving—or so they said—birth to Assyrian jugs. I also decried the claims of mediums who swore they could go through keyholes.

"What is the point of it?" I asked.

Sir Arthur became very angry. "When the great Faraday showed a stupid woman the electric spark," he said crossly, "she asked the same damfool question. Faraday replied: 'Of what use is a newborn baby?'"

I privately thought that the creator of Sherlock Holmes was begging the question, and I have yet to be convinced that there is any good in meddling in the affairs of those "on the other side." If there be such a place, then let its inhabitants, I say, remain there undisturbed.

Another amusing debate in which I took part was on the subject of Birth Control. Dr. Martin Linton Smith, Bishop of Hereford, and I spoke against it. Geoffrey Crowther and Dr. Crichton Miller defended it. The bishop, tall and splendid in episcopal evening dress, was not at ease and tried jocularly, but heavily, to capture the undergraduate spirit. It was really unfortunate when, in an attempt to recall his own stainless childhood, he found himself telling how he once "rushed from the school tuckshop clutching a large tart." This brought the house down, much to the bishop's embarrassment.

One of my happiest encounters was with Gilbert Keith Chesterton, who came to speak at a Union debate and adopted me as a sort of mascot. G.K.C. was very kind to me during his stay in Cambridge, as well as for many years afterwards. The first time we talked together he told me I was far too nervous and much too much lacking in self-confidence. It amused him to call me Gilbert the Less, flatteringly assuring me that he was only referring to my physical size.

Chesterton was a magnificent figure at the time, flamboyantly dressed with a broad-brimmed hat and cloak. It was, I suppose, in unconscious tribute to him—as well as the fact that I was going through the awful phase of reading *fin de siècle* poetry—that prompted me some time after our first meeting to buy myself a cloak with green silk lining and a slouch hat. The effect of these garments was to make me look like a replica of an advertisement for Sandeman's Port. The cloak was, in fact, a nurse's cloak. I removed the red flannel lining and had the green one stitched in its place.

This sartorial venture did not earn me half the reputation for eccentricity and aestheticism which I had hoped for. After a few weeks of parading up and down the streets with my cloak and hat brim flapping in the breeze, I felt quite hurt that nobody paid any attention. So I changed my tactics and affected a cloth cap. Caps have since returned to favour at the universities, but in my time at Cambridge they were regarded as the summit of eccentricity. I felt absurdly delighted when someone actually mistook me for Sean O'Casey.

One day, my old grandfather came to visit me at college. He was—it may be remembered—no great friend of mine. Age had mellowed him, though. He confessed that he was desperately anxious to see and hear a debate in the Union. There was, in those days, no gallery, and casual visitors were not allowed inside the debating chamber. However, I borrowed a Master of Arts gown and took the old fellow along with me, sternly cautioning him not to let me down by saying, should

I introduce him to any of my grand friends, "Pleased to meet you."

I managed to get grandfather seated in a front bench and left him to enjoy himself. Though he looked rather like a superannuated stock player in a fifth-rate tour of *Charley's Aunt*, nobody was sufficiently interested to question him or have him thrown out. What is more, when, after the debate, I introduced him to my fellow undergraduates, Lords Pentland, of Trinity, and Ennismore (now Listowel), of Magdalene, the wily panjandrum of many a provincial Masonic gathering obliged me by shaking hands with complete propriety and correctly murmuring: "How do you do."

The Chief Clerk of the Union Society, Stanley Brown, taught me a lesson I shall never forget. One day he cashed me a £5 cheque. A few days later he called me to his office and showed me the cheque with the letters "R.D." written across it. I was badly frightened. Brown firmly pointed out that a gentleman should never give a cheque unless he is quite certain that it will not bounce. No cheque of mine has bounced since that day.

Of course I was much too extravagant. It was not till I was down from the University for three years that I finished paying off the Cambridge tradesmen. But one of them I forgot. When I was in Cambridge last year I called at the pleasantly smelling tobacco shop of Messrs. Ora, in Trinity Street, to buy some cigarettes. As I was about to pay for them, the courteous gentleman behind the counter said: "By the way, Mr. Harding, we have a small account on our books which is, of course, now statute barred; but perhaps you might care to settle it now." Thus, more than twenty years after I went down, I settled what I hope is my last debt to the honest tradesmen of Cambridge.

Those were the great days of the Festival Theatre on the Newmarket Road. Run by a fellow called Terence Gray, with a black spade beard and a black Rolls Royce car, it used to draw town as well as gown with outstandingly good productions by Norman Marshall. It was also one of the first theatres to nurture the great talents of Robert Donat, but I cannot claim to have seen this fine actor there.

The place had its little peculiarities. Programmes were printed on special paper so one could read them in the dark. The ushers wore green, gold and yellow. There was an impressive cyclorama and a revolving stage. The restaurant was very good and negus was served in the bar.

I remember one night when Bernard Shaw came to see the production of one of his plays. Now, with the exception of *Saint Joan*, I am afraid Shaw's plays bore me to tears. For me they are generally far too platitudinous and patronizing. That night, in reply to rapturous applause and shouts of "author," the celebrated playwright just stood up and when the tumult subsided, said: "This is absurd. Why should I stand up and give you a free entertainment?" Later, in the restaurant, crowds swarmed round the great man. But I kept my distance. Shaw had once measured his mind against Shakespeare's and found our greatest dramatic poet lacking in Shavian intellect. That was enough for me. Measuring my undergraduate mind against the peevish perpetrator of that evening's feeble and churlish curtain speech, I was content to leave him to the sycophants flocking about his vegetarian table.

Queens' was, on the whole, a fairly quiet college. There was not a great deal of ragging. Still, there were occasional fireworks and it is interesting to look back and wonder how one could have found it amusing to break furniture, shatter diamond-paned windows with airgun pellets, or scrape one's heavy boots over mellowed walls to avoid paying a small fine for coming in late.

Despite sporadic outbursts of anger, I had not then formed my character and was, on the whole, a shy, timid boy. During the General Strike of 1926 I found that my sympathies on the whole were with the strikers and the trade unions. I did not approve of the hysterical volunteering by well-to-do and privileged young men to break the strike. My views on the subject made me unpopular with some of the extreme hearties and I learnt that there was a movement to throw me in the river. I did not relish the prospect and carefully took pains to avoid a direct encounter with the bully boys until the strike fever died down and my apostasy was forgotten.

The strike came as a great boon to a large number of rather stupid undergraduates who were viewing the coming examinations with misgiving and alarm. I often wonder if there would have been so many volunteers if it had not been known that those with strike-breaking service to their credit, or discredit, would be leniently treated by the examiners.

Among the more harmless college japes was the incident of the chapel bell. Evening services would be announced by the striking of a few chimes at seven o'clock. One evening a clever young man so arranged it that the chimes did not stop striking. To make sure of achieving the maximum amount of confusion, he locked the door leading up to the belfry. The chimes went on striking for some fifty minutes before a second key was found and the excruciating racket silenced.

Some of our jokes were in pretty poor taste, particularly on Guy Fawkes night when it was considered fashionable and amusing to put out all the town's street lamps. The final and supreme target of the night would be the lamps in the Market Square. Here the police would rally in force and the proceedings usually ended with about an equal score of jailed undergraduates and helmetless bobbies.

On one occasion I joined a group of Queens' men for an evening out at the New Theatre, where a particularly bad revue was playing. Each took with him a piece of rough calico. Whenever the poor girls of the chorus lifted their legs we ripped the calico. The manager sent for the senior proctor, now Bishop of Ely. He was bitingly sarcastic about the manners of young louts who were cruel and ill bred enough to embarrass people who, for little pay, were doing their best to entertain us. Although chastened by this dressing-down, I was nevertheless involved in more trouble soon afterwards.

52

7

AFTER attending a twenty-first birthday celebration I found myself making a speech on the Senate House steps. Liberally lacing my utterances with racy quotations and irreverent references to Town and Gown, I held forth, cheered on by my fellow-revellers while drawing many black looks from passing townsmen. This led to my appearance before Mr. Welbourne of Emmanuel. "In future," he said to me, "when you want to make a beastly nuisance of yourself, do not do it in the streets of Cambridge, but in your own college and so inflict the consequences of your presence here upon your college which is responsible for it and not on the townsfolk, who can't help it."

We used to amuse ourselves a great deal with amateur journalism. I tried to get things into the *Granta*, the leading undergraduate weekly, though I found far greater scope for self-expression at Union debates. Considering the extreme youthfulness of most of the contributors, we sometimes attained fairly high journalistic standards.

Typical of the Cambridge wit of the time is Christopher Saltmarshe's "Cavalcade for the General," *to be sung with appropriate (yet not improper) gestures by one of Mr. Cochran's Old Ladies*, which I included in my *Treasury of Insult*.

> *Our Mr. Coward's such a nice young man (such a nice young*
> *   man is he).*
> *It must be remorse for being so coarse in the days when*
> *   love was free;*
> *When private lives and other men's wives were a riot of dope*
> *   and gin.*
> *Ah, vice on the stage was all the rage when Coward and sin*
> *   came in.*

But now Mr. Coward is much too nice (such a nice young man
is he)
To shatter and vex our ideals of sex with themes
of adultery.
Now he mirrors the age on a larger stage and his people are
loyal and true,
And when they sing, it's "God Save the King" or
"Three Cheers for the Red, White and Blue."

What a change to go to a nice, clean show (such a nice
clean show, my dears),
And to see the vast and impersonal cast march past to
deafening cheers.
It's not quite art or terribly smart, but dowagers weep in
the stalls.
And I really can't see why the man next to me repeatedly
said it was *****!

The internal politics of the Union were sometimes very
funny. We had what we called private business meetings.
The biggest jape was when we found that the Union Society
subscribed a considerable sum every year to the National
Union of Students. Some of us took great exception to this.
Left wing students were all in favour of it, of course, but at
a private business meeting we secured the withdrawal of the
'sub'. Angrily the left wing boys demanded that it be restored,
and demanded a poll of the whole membership of the Society.

Though I had no political animosity towards my colleagues
of the left, I took my stand on principle on the side of those
who were against restoring the subscription. In the rooms at
Christ's of Patrick Devlin, a fine scheme was hatched. On
the morning of the poll, hundreds of men of the University
received from us two communications. One was badly written,
clumsily duplicated, and inaccurately addressed and posted
without a stamp, urging the recipient to vote for the National
Union of Students. The other, properly stamped, lucidly written

54

and properly printed, urged him to vote against the N.U.S. As a result, even those who were indifferent about the whole thing, were so annoyed at having to pay the postage on what they thought was a disgracefully sloppy communication from the N.U.S., that they turned out to vote against resuming the subscription and the poll went heavily in our favour.

My own political interests were so amorphic in those days that the first thing I did on arriving at Cambridge was to join all three political clubs—Liberal, Labour and Tory. At Queens' I belonged, to my great pleasure, to a club called The Cherubs. I can still remember how delighted I was when asked to join: for one thing it entitled me to wear a magnificent tie. The Cherubs was very exclusive, its fifteen members being made up from five students of each year.

We were a peculiar lot. The Cherubs used to meet every Saturday evening, each member taking turns to be host in his rooms. Over beer and sandwiches we had many a merry meeting which always ended up in rowdyism. We were, therefore, somewhat unpopular with the college authorities.

My dear friend, Douglas Horsley, Bishop of Gibraltar, who died recently, was a leading Cherub. The tie, which I still proudly wear, was of blue, green and pink stripes, and we also wore blazers and stockings to match. In those days, of course, we could dine for little money, and our annual dinner was always a magnificent affair.

The other club in the college was The Kangaroos. This was more sporting than dramatic. Not being at all athletic, I preferred the Cherubs. R. W. V. Robins, the cricketer, and R. R. M. Bacon, now Chief Constable of Devon, were Kangaroos—so was "Tub" (now Sir Leslie) Rowan.

We must also have talked a lot of rubbish, for it now seems that there were weeks on end when we did little else but air our unformed views on music, poetry, literature and politics. We also managed to be gay, sometimes with lamentable consequences. I well remember my first really drastic experience of the dangers of "over-fortification." It was the first Cherubs' dinner I attended. One of the members was an undergraduate older than most, a married man, ex-R.F.C., called "Charles" Chapman who afterwards as Allan Chapman became Assistant Postmaster-General. He very generously provided the drink.

We assembled in our dinner jackets and smart Cherub bow ties. I can never forget the sequence of cocktails, sherry, Chablis, claret, champagne and brandy. It was too much for me. About two o'clock in the morning I "ceased upon the midnight with no pain" and passed out in the most spectacular fashion. My friends put me to bed and did the somewhat disagreeable tidying up which was necessary. The incident gave me a sharp warning which I would have done well to heed.

Despite these occasional excesses, I was not altogether unpopular with the authorities. The two most popular dons at Queens' were the Dean, "Charley" Wood, who was always prepared to offer counsel and cocoa to anyone who cared to see him, and Archie Brown, now Vice-President, a rowing enthusiast and engineering don. Wood (still happily with us as Rector of St. Botolph's) and Brown were extraordinarily kind, and a real influence to the good so far as I was capable of learning from them.

My tutor, Laffan, who was the Chaplain, also remained a good friend throughout my three years at Queens'. He was, by the way, very High Church. "Charley" Wood, on the other hand, was Low Church. So the porter in charge of the Chapel was constantly checking which one of them would take the evening service. The poor fellow was sorely tried, seldom knowing until the last moment whether to light the candles or not.

One of the most amusing dons I knew was Gaillard T. Lapsley, lecturer in constitutional history at Trinity. He was an American who fell in love with Cambridge and became a Fellow of Trinity. He had an abhorrence bordering upon eccentricity of female students, believing in an old-fashioned way that women had no place at the university. It was about

Lapsley that the story of "the solitary gentleman" was first told.

It was his practice, irrespective of the number of women undergraduates who attended his lectures, always to address his assembly collectively as "Gentlemen." On one occasion, a classic horse race having drawn to Newmarket all of his male students except one miserable crammer, there was considerable speculation among the dozen or so girls, who had dutifully turned up from Newnham and Girton, as to how their lecturer could possibly ignore them this time. Lapsley confounded them by walking up to his desk and, gazing coldly at the solitary male student, beginning thus: "*Sir*, this morning I propose to tell you about . . ."—and embarked on his lecture impervious to the outraged women sitting a few feet away from where he stood.

This excellent fellow was, I regret to say, something of a snob. His great pleasure was to collect around him persons of title. I remember attending one of his receptions at Trinity at which the guest of honour was the Belgian Prince de Ligne. When this fine flower of the *Almanac de Gotha* arrived, Lapsley proudly escorted him to the centre of the room and said: "Your Highness, allow me to present to you *Lord* This, *Lord* That, *Lord* The Other, *Sir* Whatnot Whatnot . . . and last, and I'm afraid quite the least, Mr. Gilbert Harding of Queens'."

The American tourists who passed through Cambridge on a quick rubbernecking tour often embarrassed their resident countrymen. I used to earn extra money during the long vacation by acting as a sort of Cook's guide to visiting Americans. It was an arduous way of earning a few shillings. Once I remember taking a group of these tourists to the Great Gate of Trinity over which is a statue of the founder, Edward III. On either side of this are the armorial achievements of his sons, Edward the Black Prince, Clarence, Lancaster and several more. The last one of all is John of Hatfield, whose shield is bare of achievement because, as the pathetic legend says, *Mortuus infans*—died in infancy. "Well, say," said a bowler-hatted Baptist parson from Idaho, "I should have thought that a college with all that dough could have filled in that end shield." I made the mistake of trying to explain, but soon realized I was wasting what I had of sweetness upon a particularly desert air.

Money remained a continual problem. Much as I loathed taking exercise, I was frequently obliged to do so on Sunday mornings. For a while some of us had a habit of cycling as fast as we could after morning service to a public house a few miles along the Trumpington Road, the last arrival having to pay for drinks. Since I rarely had enough for the round I never was the last.

There were so many things one couldn't do. It irked me not to be able to go to the theatre and "flicks" as often as my richer friends. Worse still, was to feel tongue-tied and ill-informed when the latest shows were discussed. This is not to say that I was basically unhappy. Cambridge had—and has—so much to offer the young, questing mind, that I always urge parents who consult me on the matter, to send their children to the University—if the youngsters really want to go—even if their income is limited. However much their children may feel stultified in not having enough to spend, the company of lively contemporaries and the "clash of mind on mind" which is the real joy of Cambridge life, is worth any sacrifice.

A pleasanter experience of showing someone round the University took place one bright spring morning, when my charge was a man who struck me as one of the most sincere and enthusiastic people I have ever met. He was, in the best sense of the word, an impassioned orator, and I was greatly impressed by his sound sense and vigorous honesty. When he spoke in the purplest fashion about the advantages we enjoyed at the University, I felt a strong compulsion to stop lazing by the Cam and do some useful work in the docks beside the Thames. I am glad that when I met Lord Citrine again at a Colchester Oyster Feast he remembered our meeting of more than twenty-five years before.

Citrine and Chesterton between them turned me temporarily towards the Labour Party. In my second year at Queens', however, there came with one of the Universities Missions, Bishop Temple and a vigorous and violent evangelist called Nicholson. The sound and the fury of their dynamic preachings at the churches of Great St. Mary and Holy Trinity, temporarily converted me to extreme Protestantism. I gave up drinking and smoking and went to Keswick for the Convention for the Deepening of Spiritual Life. After a month or two of profound and rather pompous "spirituality" I found I was not cut out for that type of tub-thumping, after all.

Some time before, I had made my first overtures to Anglo-Catholicism. During my last, lazy months at school I had gone up to Bradford, where my mother was Matron of the Bowling Park Poor Law Institution. One day, I went off with a newspaper reporter friend to "cover" the dedication of an Anglo-Catholic chapel on the outskirts of Bradford. I found the ritual and the vestments and the incense most attractive. Somehow my attraction was intertwined with that bygone picture of my late headmaster, Lampitt, lying in his coffin in Anglo-Catholic vestments. Psychiatrists, whose business it is to understand these things, will probably infer from this that I was seeking my lost father in all this ritual. They may infer whatever they wish; all I know is that I was drawn to this form of religion and that I would have been a dull, unimaginative lout, to have resisted its attraction.

Of course, once I settled in Cambridge, the fact that my supervising tutor, Laffan, was an Anglican helped to crystallize my feelings and shape the course of my religion. But I was far too curious about everything to be a docile convert, no matter how powerful the influences around me.

I think I can claim to be the first person to burn incense inside King's Chapel since the Reformation. The Dean of King's, Eric Milner-White, being a High Churchman, and

59

the Provost being acquiescent, permission was granted for incense to be used when three African bishops came to sing High Mass in the chapel during a Universities Missions to Central Africa (U.M.C.A.) Conference. I secured the job of burning the incense and, by heavens, I burnt it. I filled the place with its pungent odours. Incense hung in clouds everywhere and you could smell it for days afterwards—to the fury of Low Churchmen like Dr. Mann who liked things done "decently and in order."

I was, nevertheless, appreciative of other religious ceremonies. What gave me more pleasure than any other Cambridge ritual was the University Sermon. Every Sunday in full term, I would watch the procession leaving the Senate House (where I had disgraced myself with that drunken oration) and follow it to the Church of Great St. Mary. On "Scarlet Day" I would be quite captivated as first the doctors, wearing their scarlet gowns and hoods, appeared, followed by the proctors and their silk-hatted "bulldogs," those beefy but fleet-footed enforcers of undergraduate rules and regulations. Then came the Esquires Bedell, also wearing top hats, but wrapped in long gowns and holding their wands of office. They would be followed by the professors and heads of houses in scarlet robes and flat velvet caps. Finally, the Chancellor and the Preacher.

Against a medieval fretwork of walls and spires, I would find myself transported into that other world of Tudor grandeur; the world of Burghley and Leicester and Don John of Austria, when Marlowe and Shakespeare were creating the springtime of our present tongue. The illusion itself was completed as I sat in my pew and listened to the glorious words of the Bidding Prayer in Cranmer's matchless English. "Ye shall pray for . . ."

Sometimes I would steal like a penitent into the magnificent Chapel of King's, which I had so effectively swamped with incense, and listen to the evening services. I am quick to tears (sometimes I cry at the pictures) and there was always a lump

At Wolverhampton Royal Orphanage School (Rev. W. L. Allen, *back row centre*).

At Queens' (G.H. *second row down, left*).

"Tobacconists were glad to let the gentlemen of

Photograph: John Bull

in my throat as I listened to the superb singing of the choir in that vast candle-lit chapel—an experience which can now be enjoyed by everyone who listens to the broadcasts from King's on Christmas Eve.

8

In my last year I had rooms in Walnut Tree Court, a place
to which I am nostalgically drawn whenever I return to
Cambridge. I now knew many people, and was constantly visiting or receiving visitors. One hardly ever had meals alone. The
day would begin with a breakfast party, and these could be
quite splendid. Since even then I loathed my own society, I
would begin each term by having enormous breakfast parties
on the strength of which I found myself being asked to breakfast for the rest of the term. Rather than face the prospect of
breaking my fast alone with tea and bread and butter with
occasional marmalade—a throwback to my loathsome
schooldays—I would order several hot dishes from the kitchen.
These would be carried up to my rooms by the kitchen porter,
and there would be appreciative roars from my guests as that
factotum whisked away a green baize cloth and revealed plates
of porridge swimming in thick yellow cream, fried fish, choice
of bacon and eggs and kidney or cold pheasant or partridge
pie. College "gyps," or waiters, would serve coffee and tea, and
the lot would be washed down with light ale, whisky, brandy
and sherry.

One day, an old Cambridge bore called Woollard, who
frequently invited undergraduates to his breakfast table,
was telling us of the vanished glories of the Victorian era.
This hospitable but tiresome fellow proceeded to explain that
things were done much better in those days because the
lower classes knew their place, gentlemen were still gentlemen,
and ladies (God bless them!) never overstepped the bounds of
modesty.

Woollard was a great admirer of Lord Palmerston, so, as
I sat eating the appetizing but plain breakfast, I remembered

62

how the statesman had towards the end of his life been given a breakfast of lamb cutlet, devilled kidney and a pint of port. Soon after this he died, regretting that he was to be removed from this world so soon after he had discovered what a capital breakfast this made.

Thereupon with some difficulty I persuaded the kitchen to provide me with exactly the same breakfast. I then invited Woollard to eat with me. My intention was to confront the old chap with such enormous helpings that he would have to refuse them, when I would tell him that he was turning down a meal which Palmerston, his hero, would have tackled with relish. To my horror, though, my ancient guest tucked into this gargantuan meal without making any comment whatsoever.

Groaning inwardly, I too ploughed through the breakfast, unable to escape from my own trap. Possibly old Woollard was wilier than I had credited him to be.

Mother used to come occasionally and express alarm at the rate of my expenditure. I heeded her not. One day someone who knew me well told her that I had many childlike qualities. Having just emerged from one of our more unsatisfactory interviews, Mother snapped: "One can hardly call them qualities and they are certainly not child*like*. To my mind they are just child*ish*."

There was a gas ring in my sitting-room, but I could never bring myself to cook on it. Any small jobs, such as boiling a kettleful of water for my tea, would be done by the wonderful old lady who acted as my "bedder," or "char" as she might be called if engaged on similar duties outside a university. This fine old soul would regale me with horrible stories of her own and her friends' operations. These would be so gruesome and so varied, that I wondered anyone in her circle had any insides left after the surgeons had done with them.

One day I discovered that my "bedder" friend was helping herself to large quantities of my tea. Being very proud of my fine Darjeeling from Matthews I filled my tin but never used it, drawing instead on a supply which I hid in a drawer. In due course my amiable "bedder" informed me that I had used all my tea.

"Impossible," I replied. "There's plenty in the tin." Whereupon the beldame showed me the empty tin.

"Then you must have used it," I told her, "because I have not touched that tin for several days." Opening the drawer, I showed her where the supplies had been coming from. Of course, she admitted taking the tea, and, of course, I forgave. It was more difficult to be magnanimous when I later found her watering my sherry after having taken a few nips from the decanter, but we remained firm friends through all our cat-and-mouse sorties.

Once, when I reached a very low watermark in my finances, I went to Newmarket with a young Irishman who had horse blood in his veins. Under his skilful guidance and direction I quickly won £18. "This," I thought as we drove the dozen or so miles back to Cambridge, "is the life. From now on I shall cease worrying and simply back horses." Inspired by greed and enthusiasm I joined my Irish friend the following day and, on the same course, under the same direction, lost £25. That finished my career as a racing expert. The most difficult thing about that experience was to pretend that I didn't mind losing. I hated it—and still do.

Still avid for excuses to spend what money I got, with Kenneth Adam, now Controller of the B.B.C.'s Light Programme, and Geoffrey Crowther and several others, I became a founder-member of the Hippolytus Club named after the Greek hero who failed to return the love of his stepmother, Phaedra. This was an amusing, insincere, anti-feminist association. Inevitably, there was a dinner. We asserted our independence of the fair sex by having the menu printed in masculine, rather than feminine French. We also handed out bachelors' buttons. We never got as far as a club tie and colours because most of the founder-members became almost immediately involved in affairs of the heart. Nearly all, as far as I know, are now married.

I was beginning to wake up, but I was still not very sure of myself. If I was at all flamboyant, it was usually—apart from such quirks as the cloak or the Senate House steps speech —in a very subdued way. It was still quite usual for me to get into people's bad books, however. I belonged to the Guild of St. Bernard and we used to have monthly communion at St. Edmund the Martyr's, the key of which was kept by the Dean of Pembroke, now Bishop of Ely. My duty was to get the key on the previous Saturday evening. Twice I forgot it and had to wake the Dean, who always kept the key with several others on a ring in his trousers pocket. Early one morning I was setting out for communion when I realized that I had forgotten to collect the key for a third time. Fearing to disturb the Dean by having a servant sent up to him, I tiptoed up to his bedroom where the reverend gentleman was still slumbering. As I groped through his clothes I found myself so agitated that the minutes ticked by and I failed to find the key. In the end I made such a clatter that I woke the Dean. For a moment he gaped, startled, at the intruder. Then he cried: "Surely, you have not forgotten for a third time, Harding?" There was nothing I could say in reply, and the good Dean sent me packing with more than a considerable flea in my ear.

This story was retold with considerable elaboration by the Bishop during a National Farmers Union dinner which we both attended at Ely.

We had one or two pleasant rags during that last year. One was the so-called opening of Tutankhamen's tomb. This archaeological phenomenon took place in the men's lavatory on Market Hill. Amid the sounds of water flushes and the cries of vegetable mongers above we unearthed from a mummy case the most remarkable collection of Egyptian relics, such as even the late Lord Carnarvon, busily grubbing among the excavations in the Valley of the Kings, would have been astonished to find.

We also opened Mother Shipton's box. At least, that was the name we gave to a commonplace antique chest. We cunningly spread it abroad that someone had discovered the personal chest of the ancient prophetess who, among other things, is said to have predicted that carriages would go without horses—in other words, cars and trains. Having collected an enormous crowd we opened the chest. Our audience was suitably impressed when we produced from it bleeding limbs (papier mâché) and domestic articles (rusty from long immersion in the river Cam). Credulity was stretched too far, however, when bits of motor tyre and railway carriage window straps emerged from this 16th century historical "find."

Among my acquaintances at that time was an American undergraduate called Sonnie Burns, who had an excess of fat and innumerable girl friends. Far from repelling them, his rotund figure attracted almost every class of girl, from barmaids and kitchen maids to the students of Girton and Newnham. (They were not then, as now, given the hideous name of undergraduettes.)

One day I was standing on Clare Bridge with Sonnie Burns, when towards us drifted a punt containing two young women, one of them a peer's daughter upon whom, being that kind of American, my corpulent friend was obviously trying to make an impression. Crying "yoo-hoo," he jumped off the bridge and landed in the punt, which immediately sank beneath his weight. As the three of them floundered in the dank, green water I gazed placidly from the bridge, thankful for once that I was not so smitten by feminine charms.

Though I did not attempt to raise a hand to rescue those idiots, I was grateful myself for a little assistance shortly afterwards. There was a mill race off the Newnham Road. It was always great fun to go up to the edge of this in a canoe and then turn round sharply and be carried down in the current. One afternoon I overturned and found myself floundering, fully clothed, in the chilly waters of the race. Gasping and bewildered, I was dragged out with a boathook.

We are, I suppose, a fairly ordinary lot. Whenever I return

66

to my old university I am alternately appalled and amused to find how repetitive undergraduate manners really are. Even the wars between Town and Gown (although Cambridge is now a city) fall into the same patterns of mistrust and resentment on both sides—in a purely localized sense, of course.

I remember there was a rather pompous young salesman in a Cambridge store who would give people offence for one reason or other. He affected the more obvious undergraduate mannerisms and at night carried a broad scarf under his arm in the hope of being mistaken for a member of the university. Yet, despite his private whim to be one of us (or perhaps because of it) he bitterly resented any undergraduate who attempted to make a purchase from him.

One day I persuaded one of my friends to go into the store and be careful to let himself be seen stealing a black chamber pot on which there were roses painted. Pretending to conceal this flamboyant article under his gown, my friend passed under the nose of the unpopular assistant. Thinking, no doubt, that here was a wonderful opportunity for revenge, the counterjumper let my friend reach the pavement and then called after him, "Stop thief."

My friend promptly bolted and the shop lad was unwise enough to give chase. This went on till they reached the corner of Jesus Lane where I was waiting with a drum and fife band. Shaking with laughter, my friend returned the ornate chamber pot to the outraged assistant, explaining that he had only intended to show it to his friends. All of us gaily agreed that this was true, so the outraged shop assistant was obliged to walk the long distance back to his shop carrying the utensil without the kindly shelter of a gown to hide it from sniggering bystanders. Whereupon I started up the drum and fife band, and we all followed him back to the shop, highly amused by our strategy. I realize now how beastly this was; but it's too late to be properly sorry.

My other brush with a townsman was due to the over-politeness of a taxi driver. Now, to my mind, there is a fawning type of politeness which amounts to downright dishonesty. This taxi driver had on several occasions taken me to and from the station. Every time I asked him what I owed him he would say in a buttery voice: "I leave it to you, sir." I found this most irritating, so when for the fourth time I asked him to tell me how much his fare was, and for the fourth time he said he would leave it to me, I gave him sixpence. The fellow immediately rushed after me, protesting that I was cheating him. Telling him to go to the devil, I went off to catch my train. The next time I rode in that man's taxi I was told exactly what I owed him at the end of the ride. Whereupon I gave him double, and we became amiably disposed towards one another.

Towards the end of my stay at the university, G. K. Chesterton invited me to lunch with him in Soho. I put off going to Bradford to see my mother in order to keep this date with my great-hearted mentor. We went to a restaurant in Charlotte Street where, with his usual zest for doing things well, he tried to teach me to eat spaghetti. We laughed uproariously at my awkwardness . . . G. K.'s laughter was always kindly.

On my mentioning that, but for his invitation, I would have been in Bradford, he asked whether I knew the Rev. John O'Connor. I did indeed know him, having met him some months earlier while on holiday. This I told Chesterton, adding that I had been greatly impressed by O'Connor's wonderful personality. Only then did Chesterton tell me that my new Bradford friend was the original Father Brown, the Roman Catholic priest whose hobby was criminology, and hero of Chesterton's *The Wisdom of Father Brown*, and other books.

Chesterton suddenly went on to say: "You, my boy, will inevitably become a Roman Catholic, too."

I went back to my college, wondering what I should do about my future. So uncertain was I in those days that at one time it had been arranged for me to be ordained as a clergyman of the Church of England. I balked at surrendering my soul altogether to Rome, so as an Anglo-Catholic I got myself accepted by the Bishop of Durham as a candidate for ordination in his diocese. The first step towards this was to go to the College of the Resurrection at Mirfield in Yorkshire. Before this, however, I had to take my degree in history.

Two things haunted my last days at Cambridge. One was the problem of what to do about my last "May Week." The other was the old, old spectre of examination nerves.

Despite the wonderful breakfast parties and club dinners, I had never been able to afford to go to any of the college balls held in "May Week," which, as everyone knows, lasts a fortnight and takes place at Cambridge in June. It is that festive time when parents and sisters and eligible girl cousins come to enjoy the end-of-academic-year "bust up," and have fun in general.

My college, with its tradition of non-extravagance, only held a May Ball every three years, and I longed to attend it. But I knew there were lean days ahead; my £250 Scholarship would shortly come to an end. I felt I could no longer live on my mother's hard-earned money. So as May Week approached I watched the great marquees going up on the college lawns and saw the gay illuminations being hung up over the bridges and by the banks of the river, and I prayed that a miracle might happen to bring me the wherewithal to go to a Ball in style.

The miracle did not happen. I could not afford the seven guineas for a double ticket, and I refused to slink in on my own and be a mere bystander or hanger-on. I did not possess tails, and lacked the hiring fee. I would have needed several more guineas to pay my whack at the champagne buffet. Altogether the notion that I, a prospective clergyman, should so desperately long to attend these revels was absurd.

So I said nothing to anyone, and managed on the whole to excuse myself from those invitations which I did receive. One night, however, as I was cycling back to Queens' from some fairly dreary meeting, I looked across the river and stopped pedalling. Against the incomparable backcloth of the great Chapel and Gibbs' Building was the King's May Ball in full swing.

Leaning on my cycle handlebars, I heard the seductive music, saw the flash of beautiful girls in lovely dresses, watched slim young men in white ties and tails escort their partners to punts moored beside the lawn, and I felt very sorry for myself. There was only a narrow stretch of river between me and the scene. As I listened to the happy laughter and heard the gay chink of champagne glasses, it made me feel very much indeed that I was a "have not."

The more pressing anxieties of the examinations had, to some degree, anaesthetized me against an excess of self-pity. For weeks I had fretted and gnawed my knuckles and lost sleep over the prospect of once more having my mind prised into by—as I feverishly thought them—hostile inquisitors determined to discover only what things I did *not* know. I had in the past got through every examination by the skin of my teeth. Now was the crucial test. I could not expect to be granted another year at Cambridge and I simply had to have a degree. My time was up; and, with my usual flair for belated remorse, I regretted the idle days I had spent, the long hours of frivolous chatter, the breakfast parties that had ruined the capacity for an honest day's work, the club dinners and sherry parties and all the other then-so-delightful and now so disenchanted frittering away of hours that should have been spent with books and pen and notepaper.

For the second part of the Historical Tripos I had to pass a paper in ancient history about which I knew almost nothing. I panicked. I contemplated the alternatives: a job as an office clerk chivvied by mean-minded seniors, a spell of labouring or being a porter, or simply a passage on a cargo ship to some outlandish port where nobody could point me out as the man whose sloth had robbed him of a Cambridge degree.

Shortly before the day of the exam I sought out a young

doctor in the Psychological Laboratory, a Dr. Buchanan.

"I'm desperately worried," I told him. "What can I do?"

"Leave it to me," said the man of medicine.

Placing me on a very comfortable couch, Buchanan told me to relax completely. After a while he told me to look up at his finger. This he held up several inches from my eyes against a strong electric light. Slowly he began to move the finger from left to right.

"Do you still see the finger?" he asked.

"Yes."

"Good. Watch it carefully."

After a minute or so, Buchanan spoke again.

"Clasp your hands," he said, "above your head."

Another minute passed.

"Now unclasp them."

I did so. This was repeated several times. Then the doctor said: "I shall now ask you to clasp your hands once again. This time you will not be able to unclasp them."

He was quite right. When he asked me to unclasp them this time I could not separate them by the slightest fraction of an inch. I was well and truly hypnotized.

Quite quietly and persistently, he said: "You are going to pass the examination and you aren't going to worry any more."

Then he snapped me out of the trance, or whatever it was that had kept my hands stuck firmly together, and I walked back to my college in something like a daze. I continued to swot, half hypnotized into a state of confidence and well laced with medicinal strychnine.

Another stroke of luck perhaps saved my skin far more effectively than that experience with the hypnotist. During one of my lapses from confidence, I told John Leathem, a great friend (now head of Taunton School), how scanty was my knowledge of ancient history.

"That's all right," he said flippantly. "All you need to

71

know is about Draco, the City States, and the Peloponnesian War."

I had only just heard of them. Patiently, Leathem explained about the Athenian magistrate who was responsible for putting the ancient laws into writing. With Draconian severity he enumerated the various city states of Hellas, with particular reference to Athens, Sparta, Corinth and Thebes. He talked to me without ceasing about the war between Athens and Sparta which ended with Lysander's capture of the former in the year 405 B.C., known to us men of learning as the Peloponnesian War.

I went into the examination room on a hot June day in an agony of apprehension. By the abundant mercy of God one of the questions was: Discuss the Draconian administration. Another question asked: Give an account of the City States. A third question commanded me to describe the Peloponnesian War. These three questions I answered, and only these three; and some time later I learned that I had just scraped through.

And so, having taken a Third Class Honours Degree in History, I went down from Cambridge.

9

AFTER the turmoil of Cambridge, I found life among the clergymen at Mirfield, near Huddersfield, refreshingly sober and tranquil. The Community of the Resurrection was founded, just over sixty years ago, by that remarkable prelate and theologian, Charles Gore. One of the authors of *Lux Mundi*, as Bishop of Worcester he was largely responsible for creating the new Diocese of Birmingham, and was Bishop there till 1911, when he became Bishop of Oxford. Mirfield is his monument: and I was indeed lucky to be sent there to prepare myself for Ordination.

I went there in the autumn of 1928, a young man without means and even less "academic" achievement. The life was quiet and semi-monastic. I soon became part of this community under a company of clergy who lived solely to preach and teach. Each night we observed the Greater Silence, and I shall never forget the restful hush of peace that followed Compline last thing at night.

On Sunday mornings, according to a peculiar but impressive rite designed by Bishop Frere of Truro, we used to sing High Mass preceded by the singing of the Litany in Procession. I remember the clergy most vividly. Among them was the son of that distinguished Bishop of Winchester of whom this delightful story is told. One day he was watching a cricket match. After one of the batsmen had welted the ball beyond the boundary, the bishop jocularly called out: "Keep it in the parish." Shortly after this another hit sent the ball towards the bishop, and it landed hard in the middle of the good man's apron. "At least they kept that one in the diocese, my lord," murmured a bystander.

It was E. K. Talbot, the least known of a famous family,

who became aware of my tendency to say too much and at the wrong time. He made me hang a text over my bed, and this I saw the last thing at night and first thing in the morning. It read: "I will give heed unto my ways that I offend not with my tongue." I often think of that and try to carry it out, but with little success.

Life was pleasant and happy. We wore cassocks and did a certain amount of domestic work. Most of my fellow-students were from Leeds University. Since I was one of a minority from Cambridge, a certain amount of mild hazing was inevitable. I found it rather bewildering to return to my cell one evening after Compline, to find that everything —furniture, clothing, books—had been removed. Eventually I discovered the stuff hidden away. It was everybody else's turn, then, to be bewildered; because, although the Greater Silence had now begun, I insisted on dragging everything back again.

While I was there, the Hostel of the Resurrection was opened at Leeds, and I went along with everyone else to attend this very grand episcopal occasion. Dr. Burroughs, Bishop of Ripon (which was our diocese), was an Oxford Low Churchman who did not find it possible to come to the ecclesiastical high jinks of the morning. These were performed by Bishop Frere. But the Bishop of Ripon *was* present during the afternoon. We all wore our hoods and gowns and, naturally, the green of Leeds University predominated. Under the circumstances, the Bishop of Ripon could not have made a more unfortunate speech.

In the presence of the Vice-Chancellor and all the dignitaries of Leeds University, he said how glad he thought he would be to find respite from his exile in the North and breathe some university atmosphere. Then, to my horror, he went on to say that Leeds, like all "redbrick" universities, could not really be more than a counterfeit of the real thing. Before the stunned audience was able to recover from this insult, the Leeds Chancellor rose and, glaring at my Lord Ripon, said he would as soon attempt to explain the glories of Leeds University as defend the British Constitution to a Hottentot. Harmony did not prevail. As we filed back to our cells and the Greater Silence, I considered myself very small Cambridge fry indeed, surrounded as I was by a hostile sea of Leeds green.

One of my great friends at the time was William Wright, known as "Father Bill." He was the extraordinarily hard-working and dedicated Catholic vicar of St. Mary Magdalene, Sunderland—a slum parish heavily hit by unemployment in Tyneside. Most of his parishioners were wretchedly poor and so was he. With Derick Sanders, a Cambridge friend, I used to go to Sunderland to help with the parish duties. One day I came to the working back-to-back house which could hardly be dignified by the name of vicarage, and found he had given away a pair of flannel trousers to someone who had nothing to wear. When I remonstrated with him, pointing out that he was probably left with only one pair himself, he quietly informed me that he had none at all. He was, in fact, wearing football shorts under his cassock. Since I had two pairs of flannels, by Biblical precept I was forced to give this saintly man a pair of mine.

By this time I had been taught theology so well at Mirfield that I found myself obliged to take their Anglo-Catholic teachings to their logical conclusion and become a Roman Catholic. A combination of influences and impressions resolved this for me. My first schoolmaster, "Dad" Lampitt, Chesterton, Laffan, and Father "Billy" of Sunderland had planted seeds which now sprouted into positive action. I left Mirfield.

Just outside Hereford, on the way into Wales, is the Benedictine Abbey of St. Michael and All Angels at Belmont. There I went to be initiated into the distinctive doctrines of the Roman Church: the seven sacraments, transubstantiation, the sacrificial aspect of the Mass, purgatory, the infallibility of the Pope and the immaculate conception of the Virgin Mary.

On June 29, 1929, on the Feast of St. Peter and St. Paul, I became a Roman Catholic.

My next problem was to find a job. This was not at all easy. My tutor, Laffan, got me an interview with some gentlemen in the City who were looking for a merchant apprentice in their business houses in Singapore and Shanghai. Nothing came of this. There was also a prospect of my getting an executive post in a canning factory, but the people in charge would not have me. So I became what I had always vowed never to become—a teacher.

The Abbot of Belmont offered me a post as lay schoolmaster at the Abbey. I taught in a gloomy, soulless room facing due north. Daylight was kept out by the bulk of the Abbey Tower, which at night racked my nerves with its incessant counterpoint of chimes. I used to have meals in the refectory and try to fit in with the monastic life. On becoming better acquainted with it, I found the Roman Catholic ritual in many ways less splendid than that of the Anglo-Catholic faith. I had fits of argument about relics and indulgences which I always found difficult to believe in.

My annual wage was £70. I was still worried about my Cambridge debts. One day I confessed these debts to a Father John Owen, who had received me into the Church. He made me hand over all my bills to him. Within a few days he passed them back to me, receipted. Did I say all my bills? This is incorrect. No one is ever completely honest about debts. Still it was a relief to learn from Father Owen that most of them had been paid by some "unknown Catholic of means." I have never forgotten the sudden release of pressure after the torment of owing this money, and it has always made me very sympathetic towards anyone burdened with debt.

Adjusting oneself to being in a monastery can be arduous to anyone. For someone of my temperament, it is near to impossible. After all, I was a layman, not a monk. I was twenty-two years old, restless, argumentative and full of strange, unresolved ideas and aspirations. I was also gregarious.

Having spent my early years in this part of the world, I knew plenty of people and found myself frequently being asked to parties. On one occasion I was invited to attend a rather grand dinner party. That same afternoon I was invited to a less formal gathering of young friends and I had been out on the loose for several hours before I returned home—which in my case was the monastery—to change into hired tails.

My return was badly timed. It was, to begin with, a Holy Day. Everyone was expected to pay special attention to his devotions. I came hurrying in by the back stairs, reeking of brandy and rum, and looking very festive, just as the monks were lining up to go into Compline. Fifty grave and tonsured men gazed sorrowingly at this deplorable sight. They looked even more sad when, on returning from their chantings, I chose to make my departure, jauntily attired in an outfit which would have been more appropriate on a tap dancer.

After an unsatisfactory year at Belmont I thought I needed a change. So I went to teach at a private school in Tonbridge, Kent. My degree was not good enough for anything more grand. The place was run by two brothers, one of whom took an instant dislike to me. So we parted by mutual consent.

My next move was to go back to the Benedictines—this time the monks of Fort Augustus on the shores of Loch Ness. From there I moved to a small preparatory school at Edinburgh which the monks had just opened. My year in this beautiful city was extremely happy. I made many Scottish friends and had a wonderful time.

This did not prevent me from wagging my tongue in anger when provoked. I remember one instance which, to me, is typical of the false rumours and downright malicious lies that are always told about any celebrated or notorious person, from the sting of which even Royalty is not immune, particularly in Scotland, where it is almost a national sport to carp if a Duke of the Blood Royal plays polo on the Sabbath or a Princess is seen smoking a cigarette in public.

77

This smallness of mind, which is the only flaw in the noble Scottish race, came to my notice after King George V and Queen Mary had attended a performance at the Edinburgh Mask Theatre of *The Admirable Crichton*. I knew the people who ran the theatre and was happy enough to vacate my seat in the front row of the circle when the management learnt that the Palace party was bigger than expected. I was, therefore, standing at the back of the dress circle when the King and Queen approached. Just then the orchestra leader, mistaking some signal, struck up the National Anthem too soon.

"Oh, dear!" I heard Queen Mary exclaim, "are we too late or are they too soon? I am sorry. Tell them that we shan't be a minute." Their Majesties then ushered their party back and put the theatre manager at his ease while the orchestra leader was instructed to start the anthem all over again when the King and Queen had been given a chance to get to their seats.

Some days later, as I was having tea in an Edinburgh restaurant, I heard some silly woman discuss this incident with considerable embroidery. According to this Xantippe, the Queen had been very angry and had commanded that the orchestra leader should be dismissed for his stupidity. She went on to berate Her Majesty for being spiteful and ungenerous and virtually implied that English royalty had a "down" on all Scots, anyway.

No longer able to endure this malicious claptrap, I told the woman that Her Majesty had said nothing of the kind.

"How can you possibly know?" she retorted.

"Because I was there when it happened."

"How could you possibly have been there?" the virago said haughtily, and returned to her toasted bun.

I said no more. But despite my attempt to keep the record straight, that woman, if she is still alive, probably highly approves the blowing up of Scottish pillar boxes bearing the letters E.R. on the strength of an imagined royal injustice.

While at the Benedictine school, I witnessed a most delightful incident. The prior was a kindly and good man but a terrible snob. It so happened that while I was there the Cardinal of Westminster, Francis Bourne, came to Edinburgh. At the prior's urgent supplication he paid a visit to the school. Now the prior and I were both ex-Anglicans and converts, and, as is usual with converts, more Catholic (at the time) than the Pope himself.

The community gathered to receive the Cardinal *ad portas*, myself, the lay master, in cap and gown, surrounded by monks and surpliced little boys. Just before the saintly man was due to arrive, we were joined, quite properly and appropriately, by Mr. and Mrs. McAlister, the housekeepers, a pantry boy called Paddy and a maid called Ruby. The prior, fearing to appear too democratic, was unwise enough and uninformed enough to send the domestics off as not being good enough in quality or position to receive someone so exalted as a cardinal. Little did he remember of Catholic humility!

When the Cardinal arrived he was first taken to the chapel to make a visit to the Blessed Sacrament. Then he should have looked at the monastic part of the house. But when he came to the refectory door, Mr. and Mrs. McAlister, the pantry boy and the kitchen maid were by the green baize door in a positive welter of excitement and respect, none of them having seen a cardinal before.

"But who are they?" said the Cardinal.

"The kitchen staff," answered the prior, beginning to move on.

"The kitchen staff?" said the Cardinal. "By far the most important people in the place."

He went over to them and spoke to them, asking what each one's name was. Finally he asked Mrs. McAlister to make him a cup of tea. The Cardinal spent the rest of his time in the kitchen chatting happily to the domestic staff.

Shortly after this I became afflicted once again with the *wanderlust*. Everything seemed to bore me. I attempted to master the Scottish game of golf. In those days I had not yet understood that one of my major handicaps was lack of strong eyesight. Somehow, I just failed to be able to concentrate on the ball. After trying time and again to drive off from the first tee, only to make a frightful mess of every attempt, I was asked by the green keeper if I would be good enough to go and practise somewhere else.

Then I met Father Bede Jarret, a Dominican, who suggested that I should go West. At his instance, the Rector of St. Francis Xavier, Antigonish, Nova Scotia, came to Scotland to see me. After our first meeting he offered me the appointment, for a year's term, of Professor of English at the university there. A few weeks later I sailed for Canada in the old *Duchess of Atholl*.

10

ANTIGONISH, which is now a large and flourishing university, was in those days finding its feet with some difficulty as a seat of learning. But from the start, the impact of Canada on me was most stimulating. As we sailed up the St. Lawrence River to Montreal, passing under the Great Rock of Quebec, I revelled in the excitement of being, for the first time in my life, in the New World.

I enjoyed every moment of the long train journey to Antigonish—by no means an easy place to reach. At the last stretch there were only two trains a day, either way. I caught the 1 a.m. from Halifax and found myself journeying into a world apart. Antigonish was almost entirely a Roman Catholic town. The Bishop's palace on the hill dominated everything and the Gaelic words *Tigh Dubh* ("House of God") seemed portentously apt.

I found the winter most exhilarating. The sea freezes in that part of the world and when the snow comes people put away their motor cars and use sleighs. Midnight Mass on Christmas Eve was enchanting, with the sleighs bobbing over the moonlit snow, the bells tinkling and lights winking.

My chief annoyance while living in Nova Scotia was the local attitude to drink I believe it is still impossible in that Province to get any intoxicating liquor without first obtaining a permit. This entitles you to buy from a Government Liquor Store one half-bottle of spirits or twelve bottles of extremely weak beer. Drinking in public is out of the question except in the beer parlours, where for ten cents a glass you can— and only if you remain seated—be served with tasteless frozen beer in a room which by law must have no decorations, no music, and precious little talk.

When I learned, furthermore, that you must not drink in hotels, except in the privacy of your room (provided you were supplied), and that if you were caught with an opened bottle in a car, you would be fined, I was somewhat daunted. After all, I was not a priest bound by laws of self-denial. I was a private individual with a right to live my life in my own way.

After a week or so, I thought I would go mad if I did not have a drink. So with a new friend, one "Chick" Chaisson, I drove nearly a hundred miles to New Glasgow, where we engaged a hotel room, and were able to buy four quarts of beer. We sat on the bed and drank the lot and then drove back again to dry-as-dust Antigonish.

I must say I found the students very backward. Some were scarcely literate. This worried me so much, being no great scholar myself, that I wrote to ask the advice of Stephen Leacock, then teaching at McGill University, Montreal. The author of *Literary Lapses* sent me a typical reply.

My dear young friend (he wrote):—

(1) Don't be impatient.
(2) Try to make them want to learn.
(3) Get them interested in a play and make them act it.
(4) Be content if you can get them to write a single paragraph in good English.
(5) Don't think too much of yourself.
(6) Don't be impatient.

Admirable advice for any teacher but very hard to follow.

I was soon called in to referee Rugby football matches between our boys and other colleges in Nova Scotia and this initiated me into North America's peculiar attitude to sport. One was expected to win at any price, including the price of sportsmanship. One day, when I was refereeing a game with a non-Catholic college, a player was injured and had to be carried off the field. I decided that there had to be a

82

"bounce-up" of the ball on the spot where the incident had occurred. Someone on the other side took it upon himself to accuse me of fixing the spot too near their goal. This was quite untrue. But at this point a ranting, raging parson rushed on to the field and began accusing me of Catholic bias, Papist cheating and general Romish corruption. When I begged him to save his eloquence for his pulpit his wrath knew no words. After a minute of helpless spluttering I was denounced as a son of a whore of Babylon and several other choice expletives were spat into my face. And all over a schoolboy game!

I found hockey—played on the ice—immensely exciting: and this helped me to overlook much of the foul play, the kicking and gouging, which seems inseparable from almost every move in this swift game. Though it was easier to forgive the outbursts of temper on the ice, I could never accept the same behaviour on the Rugby field. Nor did I like the almost fanatical way the players dedicated themselves to win by fair means or foul.

On the night before one match I was horrified to find that the team was being "got at" in quite a spectacular way. Before a blazing camp fire, a pep talk was given by one of the priests. The lads were virtually threatened with eternal damnation if they lost the match. Father McKinnie, the Rugger coach, then pitched in with three "Hail Mary's" for victory on the morrow. I was not sorry when, after all this misplaced fervour, the team did not win.

The great North American game which caught my imagination even more than ice hockey was basket ball. I loved the invigorating speed and the miraculous skill involved in keeping the ball in constant play, yet touched by the hands only. As each team tries to manoeuvre the ball into the opposing goal, tension reaches a high pitch. The goal itself consists of a net only eighteen inches wide hung from a metal ring backed by a screen. Until I went to Canada I had always considered this a soft, effeminate game. I soon learnt how wrong I was.

Of course, I dropped all the usual bricks. To refer to a woman as "homely" is a deadly insult. Yet I was constantly doing so. I soon found out that in Canada no one expects serious criticism, only praise—and lavish praise, at that. To the question, "What do you think of Canada?" there can be only one answer: "Marvellous." The same goes for Canadian arts or crafts or products in any form. Sometimes you may substitute the adjective "wonderful;" but it should be one or the other if you want a quiet life.

In 1931 I became one of the least spectacular victims of the financial crash. Before going to Canada I had borrowed £100 from my mother. After some time I got an advance of five hundred dollars. So I bought a draft for £100 which cost me exactly 486 dollars. Placing this in a stamped envelope, which I sealed, I went to the railway train which would take away my letter and bring the newspapers. So I posted my letter in the front of the train and went off to buy a newspaper. Glancing at the front page I found that we had gone off the Gold Standard, which meant that if I had waited ten minutes for the papers to arrive I could have bought my £100 draft for 320 instead of 486 dollars. I rushed back to the platform, but the train had gone.

Towards the end of my year's term as English Professor at Antigonish I began to feel restless and jaded. The manners of my students did not seem to improve, and I found it more than ever difficult to teach them anything at all. Some of the lads were quite old, almost men in fact, so I occasionally gave them a drink from my precious stockpile of liquor when they came to read their essays in my room. This was, of course, frowned upon by the authorities and the cause of not infrequent bickering in the faculty room. One day I received news from England that my mother was not in good health, and so, without protracted farewells on either side, I returned to England.

11

MY first task in England was to teach at a crammer's at Arundel under the shadow of the great castle on the hill. While I was there I lived in a rather ugly cottage where A. J. Cronin had written *The Citadel*. It did not inspire me to attempt any similar masterpieces. In my spare time I was busy getting acquainted with the mechanics of my first and only motor car, an elderly Jowett. After a few spins around the countryside, during which it seemed that every other motorist was conspiring against me, I came to the conclusion that I had neither the manners nor the temper to drive a car, and I have never touched a steering wheel since.

I found cramming much better than teaching little boys in a school, or adolescents in a university. At least the assumption is that one's pupils really want to learn to get through their exams as quickly as possible. That is why I like the word "coaching" instead of "cramming." There is a better relationship between master and pupil altogether when both are working for a common objective rather than sparring resentfully against each other.

It was while I was at Arundel that I met Hilaire Belloc and G. K. Chesterton. It was one of those unsatisfactory meetings when there is so much you wish to say and yet nothing ever comes of it. Belloc, in any case, insisted on being very grand, remaining seated in the back of a limousine, "receiving."

I wish I had seen more of Chesterton during that period. But I was shy of making approaches to great men, so I am grateful to record a visit to lunch at Beaconsfield. We talked happily through lunch and then, with some surprise, we suddenly discovered that it was one o'clock the next day. During those twelve hours we had effectively contradicted ourselves scores of times on the subjects of God, poetry, capitalism and the Roman Catholic Church. Chesterton's delightful gift of paradox was at its best and we laughed uproariously in the balmy Buckinghamshire air as we wandered (I seem to remember) through the garden, he talking, I listening, in defence of Christian morals and of the glories of human faith. As he spoke, it seemed to me that the world became a rich and good place in which to live, and something of this magic has stayed in my bones. I now know that whatever disasters may befall me, or however desperately circumstances may afflict me, I have had a brief insight into the true purpose and dignity of life. Falter and deviate as we may, there is in each of us a pinch of grace which deserves—and sometimes achieves—recognition.

When at last I was preparing to take my leave from this hospitable man, I remember saying: "I am afraid I talked an awful lot."

"Oh, no," replied Chesterton, "you are a wonderful conversationalist. You let me do all the talking, which is as it should be, young Gilbert."

I fear that I have not always since borne out the wise dictum of M. Edouard Herriot, who has defined eloquence as the art of keeping silent when you have nothing to say.

Chesterton was at that time much interested in his doctrine of Distributism, which, roughly translated, means "fair shares all round." It is certainly due to his influence that my only real political conviction is anti-Conservative without any particular label. The very word "conserve" revolts me, for it places too much emphasis on the acquisitive instinct. By all means have and hold your cherished possessions, and, if needs be, fight for a cherished ideal; but let us not become mean and frightened if we happen to have a few things that others do not possess. Let us be prepared to lose all we have, at any time, if it is inevitable that we should do so—as indeed it becomes inevitable in the end, when we are alone with ourselves and only the yawning grave before us.

I must add that, for this same reason, I cannot always wholeheartedly subscribe to the present alternative to Conservatism. Socialism, as a political and economic theory of social reorganization, is the nearest approach to a just way of getting "fair shares all round." Too frequently, though, it is obscured by party jealousies, narrow doctrinaire thinking, and a tendency to "grab." That is an inversion of the desire to "conserve." No wonder the mob, which sucks up Socialists and Conservatives with equal gusto, crucified Jesus of Nazareth and gave Socrates hemlock. There are within us black cruelties that no theology, no sociology, and no law, has yet mastered.

One day at Arundel I received a letter from the Cambridge University Appointment Board recommending me to teach for the summer school at the Ecole Franco-Britannique in the University of Clermont-Ferrand, not far from Vichy in Auvergne. Here Pope Urban II proclaimed the first crusade, and here I went for three months on a cultural crusade, spending as much time and more money than I could afford in Paris on the way.

It was my first visit to Paris and I did all the conventional things, riding on trams and buses to the obvious places. I climbed the Eiffel Tower. I knelt in the cool aisles of Notre Dame and listened to the whispering echoes. I watched the sun set over the city from that incomparable vantage point on the terrace in front of Sacré Coeur. I saw the dawn lighting the grey river, leaning on dew-wet parapets—the same peculiar dawn light that Villon, Rimbaud, Rubens, Daumier and Renoir also had seen. I tasted for the first time the unique delicacies of good cheap French cooking, and savoured the tangy, fishy soups from the South. I watched the lanterns winking in the Bois, rode on a *bateau mouche*, mingled with the students and negroes and blue-smocked workers on the Boulevard St. Michel, gazed at Leonardo's smiling enigma in the Louvre, had hot onion soup in the small hours in Les Halles, drank a Pêche Champagne in the George V bar and ate hot dogs at Morgan's.

Most of the conventional places were unspeakably dull, but a man would have to be a moron not to be moved by the beauty of Haussmann's grandly designed broad thoroughfares and that of the tumbledown houses on the Ile St. Louis. You get to know a city best when you have little money in your pocket, but I have never completely fallen for the supposed spell of Paris. Whenever I have returned from there and seen once again the green and white coastline of Southern England, I have thanked God to be back and on my way to the delights of South Kensington or Hammersmith Broadway. Paris must be a wonderful place in which to show off. I am sorry that then I did not know how to, and now that I do know it is too late and I don't want to. But that first summer visit had its charm. Perhaps a man should never go back to the most intimate *arrondissements* of the past.

Down in the beautiful Auvergne country I first became aware of the intense conflict that a few years later was to show such cruel results. There was constant tension between the reactionary Fascists and what—for want of better words —one may as well call the *Freemason "Incroyants."* It was bewildering to come from England to find people who felt so violently and spoke so passionately about politics. It was not until the fall of France that the key of this problem was provided. At the time it was distressing to find that the pious Catholics were a close, scornful and despised minority. It was also rather shocking to hear from young students bitter, blistering denunciations of the Roman Church. Yet I believe it was from that part of France that Pétain chiefly recruited his fuddy-duddy supporters while it was from the ranks of the young and contemptuous that the Maquis was chiefly recruited.

My only really painful recollection of that stay in central France is a mosquito sting just by the parting in my hair. The good and kindly physician to whom I went for treatment recommended peroxide in great quantities. "Just slosh it on," he said, airing his idiomatic English. Unfortunately, this turned me into a blond. What with the sunshine and the peroxide I became a piebald character with brown patches of hair at the front and back; all of which gave rise to considerable adverse comment, and made me really aggressive for the first time in my life.

After three months of sunshine in the Auvergne, of exploring extinct volcanoes, of listening to plaintive peasant music played on bagpipes, of tasting the clean red wines of that warm soil, I went back to England (which I did not mind doing) to a job in a small school (which I soon minded very much). It was the last time I ever worked as a schoolmaster in a Catholic private school. I quickly came to dislike the headmaster as much as he disliked me.

This narrow man certainly believed in keeping ushers in their place. It was bad enough having to take my seat among the boys while the head sat, arrogant and aloof, at his family table. It was much worse to be given the same terrible fodder as that doled out to those poor boys. At breakfast, the tantalizing smell of coffee would drift across to our table while we buried our noses in lukewarm, wishy-washy tea from an urn. There were all kinds of fine-smelling savouries which we were only allowed to sniff as we bit into our bread and margarine. Lunch was not so bad; but in the evening, when the boys had gone to bed, the staff had to be content with dreary shepherd's pie or warmed-up cold meat while, at the other end of the room, the headmaster and his next-of-kin were served with splendid five-course dinners.

Fortunately, I was not pestered out of my wits by the pupils. I had by this time learnt much about handling classes. The methods of teachers like Maria Montessori have never unduly impressed me. To overstress the development of a child's individuality is—in my opinion—unfair to the child. I have encountered more neurotics and misfits from the so-called progressive schools than from the more conventional establishments.

Children can be extremely cruel. They will winkle out a

teacher's slightest weakness and exploit it. During my teaching days I always tried to recognize each child's individual bent, encouraging his proper enthusiasms while at the same time curbing his excesses. Never did I place myself in a position where my pupils could begin to patronize me or call me by my Christian name, as I have seen some masters do to the ultimate disintegration of their powers of command. The only time I ever had trouble with a class of big boys was when I asked a notorious trouble-maker to leave the class.

"Who, sir? Me, sir? Why, sir?" he asked with dreary facetiousness.

"Because you are making a fool of yourself," I told him, "and it does not amuse me to see a lad of your age acting so stupidly." The boy did not move.

"All right," I said. "If you won't go, I will." Still the boy refused to move. So I left the classroom.

I am glad to say the others asked the offender to go out and make me come back again. Some may say that all this is merely being pompous. I do not agree. The boy afterwards thanked me for making him realize how stupidly ill-mannered he had been, and we became good friends.

Parents were often a greater problem than their young. One of my pupils was the son of a noted comedian. I did not know this until, one morning in class, the boy himself told me.

"How interesting," I commented. "It must be a very difficult job. There is nothing more exacting than trying to make people laugh."

This was meant to be complimentary and reassuring, the boy having given me the impression, by his manner, that he was socially unsure of himself because of his father's work. It was taken as an insult, however. The boy wrote complaining to his father, who in turn complained to the headmaster

"What on earth do you mean by telling the boy that his father isn't funny?" the head asked me.

"I did nothing of the kind," I replied. "All I did was to say how difficult his job must be."

"That's the same thing, surely?" asked the head.

"Not at all," I said. "I was trying to make the boy proud to have such a skilled father."

"Well, don't let it happen again," the headmaster replied, unconvinced.

Then there was the sad case of the general's son. The lad's ancestors had been in the Army as far back as the records could go. It did not occur to anyone that he did not wish to become a soldier as well. One day he confided in me that he wanted to become a veterinary surgeon. There was enough of the family blood in him to make him a horse lover. Unlike his father and two brothers, however, he wanted to do more than just ride horses. So after I heard that he failed to pass his entrance examination to Woolwich I sent him a letter in which I wrote: "I am sorry you failed. You will be better employed curing sick horses than killing healthy men."

Unfortunately for the boy, the general found my letter. A few days later I was summoned to the headmaster's study.

"Am I to understand that you are preaching seditious nonsense to the boys?" he fumed.

I asked him to explain.

"Take a look at this," he said, passing me a letter. It was from the general and couched in the most violent terms. It ended by recommending that I should be horsewhipped.

"And so you should," added the headmaster.

A few years later the boy was one of the first to be killed in action in the Second World War.

The long Christmas holiday of 1932 found me in Bradford, very depressed, and—as usual—penniless. I stayed with my mother at the Bowling Park Institution and it became my custom to go to the police courts and quarter sessions for something to do.

The law had always fascinated me. Law is the foundation of society, just as the growth of religion is the basis of human morality. The early lawgivers were, in fact, priests; and in legal and religious precepts lie the rudiments of good citizenship.

91

I had first turned my thoughts to religion. Disenchanted by the more shoddy, narrow and anti-Christian interpretations of the teachings of Jesus of Nazareth, I found myself drawn to the daily parade of the courts where humanity is to be found at its least pretentious. The elaborate shams with which men daily attempt to fool each other are meticulously ripped away —like used-up plaster bandages—under cross-examination. Any man in an English court of law is only as good as his guilt allows.

Much of my time during that cold, slushy Yorkshire midwinter was spent in the Bradford police courts. Inevitably, I made friends among the constables and officials. One day I mentioned to one of these that I was dissatisfied with my teaching work, and more than certain that I would soon be obliged to give in my notice. He said: "Why not join the police force?" I laughed at the idea. On going home, however, I found myself seriously considering the possibility. Then I met Mr. Petty, Deputy Chief Constable of Bradford, who remarked on my woebegone appearance. I told him also how fed up I was. To my surprise he suggested I become a policeman with the idea of perhaps becoming an education officer in due course. So, after a hurried visit to tell my indignant employer that I would rather pound the beat than be his slave, I was sworn in to the office of constable, vowing "to preserve our Lord the King and to be diligent in the prevention of felonies both by day and by night."

12

THE fact that the Deputy Chief Constable of Bradford City Police had invited me to join the Force did not, fortunately, entitle me to any special privileges. This saved much embarrassment, since I was a very green recruit indeed, and, therefore, something of an odd man out already. "Knowing Joe" may be all very well up to a point. Beyond that, you must stand on your own. All of which is right and just and the one good reason, thank heaven, that few mumbling mediocrities get far merely through the cunning manipulation of influential strings. Only if you have something worth offering is there any point in petitioning "Joe."

What had I to offer? Precious little, except my willingness to learn. Taking it for granted that I would ultimately become something very high at Scotland Yard, I applied myself diligently to the preliminary training. I never found out what process of screening or educational tests my fellow recruits went through before they were accepted, but I do know that many of them were exceptionally bright. We all had to attend classes in English, including grammar, dictation and police law. Most of it was pretty puerile, and I sometimes found myself exchanging winks with other newcomers, to the annoyance of our bullet-headed instructor. After attending lectures in English by Sir Arthur Quiller Couch, I am afraid I found little stimulus from listening to these painstakingly prim homilies on elementary grammar.

We used a textbook written by a man called Moriarty. It is of no great academic importance to record that I averaged 98 per cent in the weekly examination, because the subject was always insignificant and the competition negligible. Sometimes I deliberately forfeited the odd 2 per cent in order not to appear too much like the Child Christ in the Temple.

Great importance was attached to the smartness with which we stood up when our instructor entered the room. It seemed ridiculous even then: and I never could bring myself to leap up like a scalded cat merely to gratify the vanity of a petty disciplinarian. It is a wonder that I got any marks at all.

My first experience of wearing uniform was unpleasant. For years I had slouched about quite happily in flannels or comfortable suits. In those days police uniform was even more stuffy than it is now. For days after I donned it I could not get accustomed to the fact that my uniform automatically set me apart from my fellow men. If, while travelling on trams, I attempted to pass the time of day with someone in the next seat, or merely to discuss the political situation in Manchuria, I found the other person coughing nervously and turning quickly to contemplate the multiple stores and warehouses of beautiful Bradford. I now realize that, in those days, many people were alienated from the police as the result of hearing the threat, as children, that the policeman would take them away if they did not eat, or wash themselves, or in some other way fail to please their inane elders. This cowardly form of intimidation is not so rampant now, but there are still foolish parents who damage young minds with such vicious talk.

There is nothing more horrible in the way of headgear than a policeman's helmet. It took me weeks to accustom myself to peering out from under this clumsy, ugly piece of uniform, and sudden glimpses of myself while wearing it were quite unnerving. I was also obliged, in my journey between the Police Station and the Bowling Park Institution, where I lived with my mother, the Matron, to carry a nasty little regulation issue attaché case, a piece of equipment as unsightly and ridiculous as the word itself. These (I cannot bring myself to repeat the grotesque name) mock-leather cases contained our gym clothes. Every afternoon we had drill and P.T. The drill was on the Guards plan. Our instructor being an ex-Guardsman, we had, as he never ceased to tell us, to step lively. He delighted in showing off, and took particular pleasure in humiliating people like myself whose reactions to command were, owing to lack of practice and excessive fat, rather slow.

"Pick 'em up, Harding," he would yell when my knees were already brushing my chin.

"Look lively," he would bawl after having done his damndest to knock all the life out of me.

I remember one occasion on which, having failed to form fours (or was it threes?) I was obliged to double up and down a fire escape until I was physically sick with exhaustion—unfortunately not on him but on me.

The "gymnasium" (the quotations marks are important) was a filthy room near the stables and thick with dust. There we bounced along on mats or swung and swayed on horrible bars. To help us to get clean afterwards, one small washing bowl of lukewarm water was provided for the thirteen recruits.

During this period of training, which lasted for thirteen weeks, a small and quite silly accident occurred. The fact that I dislocated my patella, or split a cartilage, seemed a small matter at the time. At worst, it should have meant a short spell of "light duty." As it turned out, it was to terminate my career as a policeman almost before it had started. The accident itself was due to the pig-headed obstinacy of my instructor in the first place.

In vain did I protest that I was too unpractised to be compelled to vault over a leather-covered stool known as a horse, and for once I proved to be an accurate prophet of woe. Half-leaping, half-scrambling, I heaved my not inconsiderable weight over this contraption only to find myself in a pain-racked, crippled heap in a cloud of dust on a dirty mat—and I have been something of a cripple ever since.

That meant working in the office, which is what I believe is known as a "cushy" job. But it had its drawbacks, the worst of them being that I was disqualified from going on full-time "beats." Now this might seem like a Godsend for anyone with my deep-rooted aversion to all forms of healthful exercise.

95

It was nothing of the sort. Only constables who had completed at least three years on the beat were considered for promotion. That meant good-bye to my dreams of becoming a Scotland Yard detective.

The other drawbacks were less drastic, but most irritating. It is generally assumed that any man sitting behind a desk and carrying out some menial task is fair game for anyone's bad manners. One day a motorist entered when I was on duty and asked for a HORT 1, otherwise Home Office Road Transport Form No. 1. This was a certificate of insurance of some kind. I was "taking his particulars" (a phrase which always struck me as describing some major surgical operation) when he suddenly remarked: "You speak good English for a policeman."

Looking up from my writing, I replied: "Well, for a medical practitioner you don't do so badly yourself." The fool went off and complained and I was reprimanded for insolence!

Though I was never put on point duty, when my injured leg began to heal I was allowed to take my turn on night shift. During the training period I had already been sent round for two hours every night with older policemen to learn the ropes and to be initiated into the innumerable tricks of the trade. I soon discovered there was nothing romantic about the unspeakably dreary night work which all constables endure, year after year.

Incidents, once pub crowds have been sent home, are rare. Only occasionally is one asked the way. If anyone does happen to be going along the same road as you he usually takes care to give you a wide berth or, at best, call out a hasty, "Goodnight, constable" and move on at the double. This attitude to the police is deeply ingrained in the public mind, and I must say that few constables encourage lengthy exchanges of familiarities. It is not the thing to do.

Padding around the outskirts of Bradford between midnight and eight o'clock in the morning can be wearing to anyone's temper. Mine was not always at its best. I remember how once, about an hour before dawn, a motor car containing a party of revellers stopped and asked me to put them on the right road for Leeds. I was in an unfamiliar district and not at all sure how best to direct them. Just as I was working this out, one of the merrymakers peered from the car and said: "You know something, lads? This feller isn't a policeman at all." I pretended to ignore this.

"No wonder the blighter doesn't know the way," said another inebriate.

"No kidding, pal," the driver said to me. "What do you think you're playing at, all togged up in that copper's outfit?"

"Eee, have yer bin to a fancy dress ball, luv?" asked one of the womenfolk.

"You get back int' car," warned a protective voice and the pinchbeck Gracie Fields was pulled back from the open window. "He might be a lunatic for all we know."

"Don't talk such absolute rubbish," I snapped.

"Hark at the way he talks," one of my tormentors jeered. "All lah-de-dah."

My mind was torn between the hope that a fellow constable would come to my rescue and the fear of his catching me in this predicament if he did.

"Come on, kids, we're wasting our time with this chap," another woman's voice said.

"You're right," said the driver. "He's much too fat to be a copper."

Just then one of the drunks leaned out in an attempt to tug my moustache. Floundering and shouting: "Let's see if it's real or not," he almost fell on to the pavement. This would not do at all. Pushing the man back into the car, I told the driver: "I'll give you exactly five seconds to get the blazes on your way. If you don't step on it I'll arrest the lot of you."

My voice must have carried some conviction, for without another word the driver started his engine. I puffed out my chest and thought I had done pretty well, after all. But as the car began to move off I heard one of the women say querulously: "That chap must have had a rare old do at that fancy dress party. He's raving drunk!"

One of my tasks was to "try off" property. That means testing doors and lock-up premises to see if there is any insecurity. If there was, then back I would have to trudge to the nearest police box to find out to whom the premises belonged. I would telephone to wake him and tell him to make his place secure.

This always struck me as an appalling waste of time. People who were careless enough to leave their property unfastened at night deserved anything that was coming to them, thought I. After two or three turns on the beat, during which I found everything safely locked and barred, I just went on my blithe way, gazing up from time to time at the heavenly bodies winking in their dark canopy. A tap on the shoulder interrupted my aesthetic contemplation.

"Now then, me lad," said a thick-set police sergeant. "You can gaze at the stars all you want to on your night off. Anything to report?"

"Nothing, sergeant."

"Have you tried off all the property on this beat?"

"Yes, sergeant."

"Are you sure?"

"Yes, sergeant."

"Then," roared the sergeant, "what in the name of blue tarnation is that warehouse doing with its front door undone?"

Grabbing me by the arm, the infuriated officer propelled me like a felon to the scene of my crime. Fortunately, nobody had broken in, and I escaped being "put on a fizzer," which meant being reported to the Chief Constable and also fined a sum of money.

During my entire police career I made only one arrest and that was with the help of someone else.

I believed, and I still believe, that the police forces of this country are as fair-minded and able a body of men and women as can be found anywhere in the world. The way in which they maintain law and order is magnificent. But in order to make it a vocation, one must deliberately stifle the more human aspects of personality and, in fact, reduce one's vision of the world to a rigid and narrow view. This frequently creates the finest kind of discipline, a discipline as devoted and dedicated as that of the monastic orders, or of the best type of public servant. But there is little scope for complexity of thought or idiosyncracies of character. I had already seen too much of society to be able to accept, without resentment, the more noticeable shams and prejudices essential to "keeping up a front." It is for this same reason that I know I would never have made a good doctor. I loathe and detest the mumbo-jumbo of the medicos, the hypocrisy of a bedside manner. If I knew someone was dying, and it was my business to tell him so, I would out with it and not fool the man with phoney platitudes that were outmoded before the world had heard of Hippocrates.

One of the strictest rules of the Bradford City Police Force was that you should never stop a motor car and ask for a lift home—even at the punitive hour of two a.m. There was one policeman who was always in trouble. Since he is probably still alive let us call him "Jobbo." If he had not been such an engaging and witty character he would most likely have got the sack. As it was, he had suffered every penalty known to the law.

Jobbo, at this time, always finished work two hours after midnight, about the worst time to find any kind of transport to take him home. He lived some way from the centre of Bradford, and after signing off he had to find his own way home which took him up Nanninham Lane, a steep hill on the way to Ilkley. As he was puffing wearily along he heard a car behind him. Quite cheerfully he stepped into the road and stopped it. The driver was a nervous young man who called Jobbo "sir." Now, no one calls a policeman "sir" unless he is a criminal with a guilty conscience. Thus reasoned Jobbo, but he bided his time.

"I'm sorry to trouble you," he said, "but could you give

me a lift? I have to get to a place further down the road in a bit of a hurry."

"Certainly, sir," said the driver. "Anywhere you say."

So Jobbo got into the car and directed the boy straight back to the police station. Grabbing the now thoroughly frightened youth, he marched him in just as the Halifax police were putting out a "stop and detain" warning, describing a young burglar who had escaped in a stolen car. The Bradford police were able to say, almost before the message was finished, that they had both the man and the stolen car.

When asked how he had spotted the miscreant, Jobbo innocently replied that he thought the man was driving in a suspicious manner. This apparently convinced the Chief Constable. Jobbo got all the credit for capturing his man, was commended by the quarter-sessions, and promoted to acting sergeant. But not for long. A few weeks later he was demoted for thumbing lifts home.

Once, during a tremendous snowfall, I was going on duty one evening, when a miserably ill clad boy asked me for a match.

"What for?" I said.

"To light a candle," he said.

"Whatever for?"

"To get into that house," he replied, indicating a dark, empty house looming out of the twilit snow.

Thinking the boy was a mental case, I decided to humour him.

"Is there any particular reason for wanting to get in at this time of night?" I asked patiently.

"Yes. I want to collect some furniture."

Now I knew—or thought I knew—the youngster was mad, and I told him that this seemed both a most unlikely story and an improper expedition in such foul weather.

"My father will beat me if I don't go on with it," said the boy.

"Of course he won't," I said.

"You don't know my father," the boy whimpered.

So thinking of the Children's Act and wanting better advice I told him to come back with me to the police station.

"But I haven't done nothing," the boy protested as I took his arm and started walking through the snow. Just then a tram came along.

"Hop on," I told the boy, and as the tram moved off through the slushy streets, some instinct told me to avoid making this seem like a real arrest. So I sent the boy upstairs while I remained downstairs, where I could keep an eye on anyone boarding or leaving the tram.

The lad seemed grateful for this concession and when the time came to alight he joined me quite happily. I explained that I was not arresting him, only checking on the best means of helping him.

"That's all right," the lad said. "My dad will explain everything."

Unfortunately, on our way into the police station we ran into an officious idiot in what he misguidedly thought were plain clothes. The fact that he was C.I.D. inspector stood out a mile, which was approximately the length of his copper's boots. This charming busy-body asked me what it was all about and I made the mistake of telling when, as a uniformed man, I should have reported direct to the uniformed inspector.

"Have you charged the boy?" asked the C.I.D. man.

"No. I only want to check on his story."

"Nonsense. He was obviously loitering with intent to commit a felony."

"Then why did he come up to me and ask for a match?"

"Don't answer back," snapped the detective. "Come on, we'll see about this."

There must have been a feud between the uniformed and the plain clothes inspectors, for the next thing I knew was that the C.I.D. man was telling my inspector that he should never be in charge of constables.

"You let a man like this," he fumed, pointing at me, "gaily

arrest some young sneak thief without knowing the first thing about procedure. The fool hasn't even charged the boy."

For twenty minutes the two inspectors wrangled while we sent for the father at an address given by the boy. Both policemen seemed more intent on "getting at" each other than on checking my story, so I let them get on with it. Eventually an angry-looking little Yorkshireman stumped in and, glancing at the boy, asked what we were doing. On being informed that he had been caught at the point of breaking into an empty house the man turned fiercely on the boy and said: "Is this true?"

"No, dad," the boy replied. "I was just trying to get into our old place and pick up the things you told me to collect."

"Where did you say he was trying to break into?" the bantam fighting-cock asked us. We told him the address.

"Of all the barmy people I've ever met I think you coppers are the barmiest," the man stormed. Then he began to laugh. "That's rich," he cackled. "Wait till the lads hear about this little joke."

He then explained that he and the boy had moved to another home but that there were still several possessions left in their old place. The boy had been sent to collect some of these, and I had come upon the scene at the point of his trying to do so. Grabbing his son by the ear, the cocky little man stalked out of the police station without another word, leaving three extremely discomfited police officials of whom I was the least put out.

Still, the C.I.D. man had the last word. An hour later I was instructed by a red-faced uniformed inspector to fill in a "refused charge" form saying that I had "taken him into custody on suspicion of being a person loitering with intent to commit a felony." This I was told was to "protect me." Perhaps it did, because I never heard any more about it.

Police jargon creates a world of its own. A policeman never goes anywhere, he *proceeds*. He never *watches* anyone, he has them *under observation*. Upon proceeding *to the place in question* (never the place) he keeps *individuals* (never people) under observation. He then *forms certain conclusions* and *takes the appropriate action*. Having spent the past three years and more teaching young dunderheads, I was now being taught by dunderheads myself—and not such young ones either.

There was, of course (as always), a leavening of nice honest human beings in the force. I have long maintained that there are far many more pleasant people in the world than objectionable ones, and I have not yet been proved wrong. It is only the crass stupidity of most people that obscures and distorts their innate goodness.

One man, in particular, was always considerate towards me. This was Sergeant Salter, an ex-Guardsman, who presided over the police stores. Being the man who issued the uniforms he was the first police sergeant I encountered, and his amiability gave me a completely false picture of the camaraderie in the police force. It impressed me considerably, when I complained of having been carelessly fitted out, to see this sergeant scrupulously rummaging about until he found something more suitable.

His room was the warmest spot in the entire police station, so it was always a pleasure to go there with some new complaints and warm oneself while the good sergeant slowly and carefully attended to my wants. In the end, of course, he saw through the ruse and forestalled my further demands for Savile Row service by inviting me to drop in at any time.

Food, as well as warmth, was available in this cosy hide-out. Salter fascinated me by the regularity with which he would take lumps of cold meat off the table which served as a plate and pop them into his mouth on the point of a very sharp penknife. He never seemed to stop drinking tea, and he also had a stock of savoury titbits which he kept in a small corner cupboard. Since he was full of reminiscences and was a great master of gossip, I still think of the hours I spent in his company as the most fruitful of my career as a policeman.

Fortunately, I was never given some of the really unpleasant police jobs. One of the tricks was to get young recruits into plain clothes and send them off to a public house. They would then try to persuade the licensee to serve them a drink a few minutes after closing time. If the landlord fell for the trick, the plain clothes lad would then call up a uniformed constable, handily stationed nearby for the purpose, and the licensee would be summoned. Though I was the newest of new recruits, no one ever sent me. I was too well known in the Bradford pubs!

Still there were enough minor irritations to keep me fuming —saluting for my pittance, for instance, at the weekly pay parade. For the privilege of wearing uncomfortable headgear, trudging about the streets at all hours in atrocious boots, and subjecting ourselves at all times to the pettifogging rules of a soulless administration, we were paid fifty-five shillings a week. This was bad enough, but in order to get it we had to line up and salute for it. This humiliating piece of Victorian pomposity often made me feel like telling the pay officer to keep his shillings. This, it was pointed out to me by timid colleagues, would have been a great breach of discipline. So, like Pooh Bah, I allowed myself to be insulted weekly for a handful of shillings.

One unwritten rule of the police is never to interfere between a man and wife. It is often easy to forget such rules and one evening I was found in the street by an angry woman who asked me to help her. She said her husband had been knocking her about and had locked her out. Most unwisely, I went back with her to the horrid, squalid lodging house where she lived, and began to remonstrate with the boyish lout who opened the door to my policeman-like knock.

"What do you want?" asked the scowling young husband.

"I hear that you have been hitting your wife," I said sternly.

"What if I have?"

"What if you have!" I exclaimed angrily.

"Aye, what if I have? What's it got to do with you?"

104

"I think it's disgraceful."

"Beat it, copper."

"This won't do," I said. "You have assaulted your wife by beating her."

"Didn't I tell you to beat it?"

"I shall have to arrest you."

"You'll have to what? Arrest me? I haven't committed any offence."

"I shall arrest you all the same."

"You go ahead and try," screeched a voice in my ear. To my astonishment I found the wife glaring furiously at me.

"But——" I began.

"Never mind about the buts," yelled the wife. "You heard what he said, didn't you? Well, go on and beat it." I was about to protest when the couple closed in on me and began to push me out of the house. So I took their joint advice and beat it.

As the months passed I felt more and more dissatisfied. My leg never really healed and after several hours of trudging my beat I would have to pull off my boots and socks and hold my ankle under a cold tap. I knew also that I would never get anywhere in the police force. No matter how diligent I was, or enthusiastic, when I first entered, I soon realized that I was not cut out, as they say, for the job.

Not only did I resent being summarily ordered about by others, but I was appalled by the prospect one day perhaps of reaching a position which would entitle me to do the same. I never like getting things through intimidation, or by reason of holding some position which gives me an unfair advantage over anyone. I find it easy enough to get my own way, without having to resort to bullying or hiding behind some trashy pose of authority. If I want anything done I ask for it to be done. If the person I ask is unable to do it, then all I want to see is the back of him, for he obviously has no business to be around. If, on the other hand, he carries out my instructions carelessly, I claim the right to call him a fool for not managing to do that which he pretended to be able to do. When a man actually does what he is expected to do, and does it well, I am overjoyed and shower him with praise and whatever financial reward is due to him. But at no time would I wish to carry out these transactions from behind the protection of some uniform, or through exploiting some special privilege which might be mine. There is no one I respect more than a man who will stand up to me in fair and square argument, provided he really knows what he is talking about and can make a good case for himself, which all too few people seem able to do.

Though I did not miss, as I thought I might have done, the so-called higher things of life such as books, good wine, well-cooked food, music, agreeable conversation, I found that as I became progressively more immersed in police routine, I was correspondingly duller in mind. After a spell of duty from between, say, 10 p.m. to 6 a.m. I had no time for anything except sleep. I would swallow the fine breakfasts which my mother prepared for me without being able to taste them. Then I would clamber up to bed, fall like a log into the sheets and stay there till it was time to get up, swallow some tea, clean my buttons, badges and boots, and start all over again.

Living at home had its disadvantages, the chief of these being an almost unbearable sense of distress about living on Mother. Although I paid her—or rather the institute's guardians—twenty-five shillings weekly for my room and board, I sometimes felt I was an awful drag on her. She was, after all, extremely busy. As Matron there were incessant calls on her and yet she still found time to look after me as if I were a prince. It seemed unfair, but I was usually too tired to do anything about it.

Another source of private shame was that while I was ridiculously pounding the beat as a music hall bobby, my sister Constance was establishing herself as a school teacher. I had not seen much of her after I left my childhood home at the Hereford Workhouse to attend school at Wolverhampton. But I was constantly aware of her and, in fact, closer to her in some ways during our absences than when we were together—when we invariably squabbled.

Connie had stayed at Hereford after I was sent to school. When Mother took up her appointment at Bradford during the early nineteen-twenties, Connie remained behind with our grandparents until she won a scholarship to the Teachers' Training College at Bingley, Yorkshire.

This was fairly close to Bradford and I occasionally saw something of her, but by the time I joined the Bradford police Connie had heard of a vacancy in a school at Richmond and had gone there to teach. The fact that she was settling into a worthwhile profession, self-contained, self-sufficient, and not in any way reliant on Mother, gave me not a few bad moments of conscience. "Where," I would ask myself, "are you heading? Was all Mother's effort to send you to Cambridge and equip you for a place in life to amount to a policeman's lot, and not a particularly good policeman, either?"

Sometimes I would tax Mother with this. "I'm just wasting everyone's time," I would say, as from my bed I watched her systematically tidying the kit in my room. As a result of my friendship with Sergeant Salter, I seemed to have acquired an extraordinary amount of kit. I had three tunics, five pairs of trousers, two greatcoats and several pairs of thick clodhopping boots. Always my mother reassured me. "Don't worry about it," she would say. "It's nice to have you at home. Besides, you seem more settled. You haven't run into any more debt and you've kept completely out of mischief for months. I'm not complaining." And so I would go back to sleep while Mother quietly picked up my tunics to clean the buttons.

Routine at the police station was becoming increasingly duller and less intolerable. Intellectually, I had mastered the rudiments in a few weeks; now I wanted to go on to other things, yet I was merely marking time. The fact that I was something of a misfit in a practical organization was brought home to me by a small, but significant, incident.

It had been raining all night and when my relief arrived I left the desk where I had been on duty with a sigh of utter weariness. I thought of the long tram ride back to Bowling Park, and groaned. "It's raining cats and dogs still," my colleague said, shaking his sodden greatcoat against the stove.

I grunted I know not what and went off to collect my own coat. When I was ready to leave I stood for a moment in the entrance hall, contemplating through a window the dreary brown Yorkshire downpour. Then I went towards the door.

"Be careful now, professor," a voice called out. "Don't you think you should have brought your umbrella?" Turning, I saw the jeering, grinning faces of two young constables who had joined the force several weeks after I had done. There they stood, completely at home, completely indoctrinated in their trade, while I, a pudgy, limping oddity was given the mocking label of "Professor." The fact that I was, in truth, a professor did not console me. But I was too tired to answer back. "*They* are right; *I* am the odd man out," I told myself as I went out into the rain.

My one weekly rest day was spent at home in a complete and glorious inactivity of mind and body. One day I was lolling in a delightful coma on my bed when I looked out of one eye and found my mother standing over me in a state of great excitement. I snapped into wakefulness.

"What is it?" I asked. "Good news or bad?"

"See for yourself," said Mother handing me a cablegram.

It contained the offer of a job as English master at the Greek Gymnasium at Limasol. I was flabbergasted. During the period when I was unhappy as a schoolmaster I applied for every kind of job without success. One of these futile applications had got so far as an interview. This was with the Director of Education of Cyprus, then in London with the intention of filling the post mentioned on the cable. He obviously found someone else and I forgot the whole thing. Now the vacancy was open again, and I did not hesitate.

"Mother," I said, springing from the bed, "I am not going on the beat any more."

Nor was this a false prophecy. To my great joy I was allowed to resign without much difficulty. There was such a scurry and flurry of getting my things together that I had little time to enjoy the sense of release and relief with which I handed back to Salter my uniform, boots, notebook, truncheon, handcuffs —and Moriarty.

The cable arrived on a Wednesday. By the following Wednesday I was in Cyprus. In my trunk was a parchment signed by the Chief Constable of Bradford stating that during my service as a constable in that city my conduct had been exemplary.

13

"CYPRUS," I said childishly elated as the train pulled out of Bradford's grimy station, "here I come." So anxious was I to reach my new appointment that, although I could not really afford it, I travelled to the island by the expensive overland and short sea route, rather than idle away time on the more economical sea passage from Southampton to Port Said.

Stopping in Paris (which I like) only to register my heavy baggage for Trieste (which I loathe), I raced down to the Italian port and embarked on the *Martha Washington*, a comfortable boat on which I had secured for myself one of the best cabins. I remember how the booking-clerk had stared at my poor scholar's cuffs when I inquired the price of a really good first class cabin.

"The second class berths are very comfortable," he said patronizingly.

"I didn't ask how comfortable or uncomfortable the berths are," I exclaimed. "I only want to know which cabin is better than any other. If you can answer this question truthfully, for heaven's sake do so and let me reserve it."

Impoverished as I was, I had already made it my principle to get only the best of whatever was going. It is this meek acceptance of other people's advice that is ruining the spirit of so many so-called civilized people. Only by insisting on the best (if you are reasonably able to pay for it), are you likely to maintain any kind of civilization at all.

The sea voyage was delightful. To my great pleasure, I quickly found congenial company in the persons of Christopher Sykes, now with the B.B.C., and a French lawyer whose name, I regret to say, I have forgotten. Down in the hold, travelling steerage, were a large number of Jews, the vanguard of refugees from the Hitler terror on their way to the Holy Land. On the Sabbath day, the venerable old Rabbi who was with them conducted a service. The wonderful melody of those Jews, rising into the evening air as we steamed along the impressive Yugoslavian coast, was most touching. The sad harmonies of their ancient chant increased my already strong loathing of totalitarianism and racial prejudice.

We arrived at Larnaca in the damp heat of August, a heat so frightful, so crushing, so completely flattening, that one is quite incapable of doing a stroke of work till one gets used to it. I was met by the island's Director of Education, Mr. Cullen, who, I was relieved to find, understood my discomfiture perfectly. The first thing he said was: "You'll need a week or two to get used to this heat." The next thing he said was: "I strongly advise you to spend a few days in the mountains. It will help you to get to know the island." This suited me very well indeed, for my French lawyer friend had told me that he intended to hire a car in which to tour around the mountains. When I told him I was free, he generously asked me to join him, and within a few hours we were off on one of the most beautiful trips I have ever experienced.

We soon left the vile heat of the towns and reached the hills, driving through Platres and Saitta to Troodos, known locally as Mount Olympus, six thousand feet above the dry scorched plains. There were trees and waterfalls and it was always cool. The Colonial Government had moved up there to escape the heat, and we found several big hotels for rich Egyptians where the food and service were very fine. The Governor lived in a place called Government Cottage which resembled a Chislehurst villa. Rumour had it that it was built by the poet, Rimbaud. I hope this is not true.

We then drove down to Famagusta, a fine walled city in the north-east of the island. We explored Othello's Tower and the great Mosque, a savage, round-bellied architectural eruption. It was here that I discovered that Shakespeare was mistaken in making his Othello a black man. The original Othello was a Venetian nobleman called Christofo Moro during the time when Cyprus belonged to Venice. Moro was no more a black man than Henry Moore of Yorkshire. But what sublime dramatic poetry was fashioned out of the Bard's schoolboy howler!

At the far tip of the island we reached the Monastery of St. Andrew. It was wonderful to look out over the orange plantations then sprouting up in the hands of refugee Jews. Driven out of their homes by Hitler, they had come to this arid plain and, by skilful irrigation, had made the desert blossom like a giant orange tree.

We went to Kyrenia, a place of pure enchantment, where we stayed at a great hotel, called the Dome, built by a Greek named Catsellis. The glory of this part of the island was the Palace of the Lusignan Kings from which you get an incomparable view looking across the Mediterranean narrows to the great Tauros mountain range in Asia Minor.

At Kykko, we met the Orthodox Greek monks. These holy men, with their long hair and beards and black pot hats, were extraordinarily dirty but very pleasant. Always ready with refreshment, they would pass you countless little cups of coffee and succulent sugar plums stuck on the ends of forks. As I took my ease in this Attic ancient world, I found it hard to believe that less than a fortnight before I had been pounding the beat as a Bradford bobby.

At last, I reported for duty at the Greek Gymnasium in Limasol. There I began teaching the boys English—a hopeless task since very few of them liked the language, or England. This was shortly after the trouble and unrest, caused largely by religious discord, which had led to the abolition of the legislative council. My pupils were very much under the influence of Enosis, the movement desiring union with Greece. They wore brown uniforms and had numbers and wore an owl on the front of their caps to remind them of Pallas Athene, Goddess of Wisdom. Tempted as I was to tell them that their militant outlook could only be a travesty of wisdom, I kept quiet until I was able to size things up better.

I soon learnt that there was no point in playing the heavy English colonial administrator. My job was to teach these recalcitrant, but basically nice Greek lads English and, by heaven, I would do just that! I had been introduced to the pupils by my predecessor who had completely failed to understand English. Calling a boy to introduce me, he would say: "How you called and how old you are?" This at least produced an answer, whereas my questions: "What is your name? How old are you?" met with blank stares.

I cannot pretend that I found it amusing to teach English to such unresponsive pupils but I got on well enough with my colleagues, and soon collected a few friends. My employer was the School Board, which included the local mayor, Hajipavlou. Anyone who has been to Cyprus will remember his brandy which, in those days he sold at two shillings a bottle. Haji and I would yarn for hours over his good liquor.

One day I told the Mayor that Cyprus was the most civilized place I knew when it came to taking a gentle drink in perfect surroundings.

"What's more," I said practically, "it's so cheap."

"Ah, my friend," smiled he, "that is because there is no tax on alcohol. But milk and water are taxed."

"That is exactly my point," I said, rinsing my mouth with brandy. "Wine is cheaper than water."

Sometimes I would sit in the cool evenings with Haji and two other friends, a man called Kakoyannis and a priest whose name I forget. This holy man was the Exarch of the Greek Church, the "Holy Exarch" we called him, and he was the cleanest Greek Orthodox priest I ever met. He paid scrupulous attention to his toilet and, unlike his charming but greasy brethren, always combed his beard.

By having friends among the local community I do not mean that I went native. My work introduced me to a colourful group of native islanders, but it also entailed a certain amount of social life in the English colony. The English Club, to which everyone from the mother country belonged as a matter of course, was pleasantly situated on the sea shore with a large verandah going out over the sea. I used to play bridge and poker there.

Sometimes we would play all night. My particular friends were Canon Newham, a married couple called Stone, and a Mrs. Gallagher. The doyen of the club was Colonel Gallagher, ex-Chief of Police. I quickly managed to get in the bad books of that martinet. One day I was complaining heatedly about Mussolini locking people up without a trial. The rest of the club piously condemned the Fascist dictator's methods.

"Mind you," said a diehard, "that chap's done a lot of good. Smartened the country up no end. Have you driven along their new roads?"

Then I went, as it was afterwards put to me, "a bit too far."

"Naturally, you people would approve of Musso," I said. "After all, you're not much better here, are you?"

This was a sore point. Since the religious and political agitations, everyone had become less tolerant towards native law-breakers.

Colonel Gallagher rose angrily. "Get out of the club, sir," he thundered. "We want none of your nasty, snivelling, long-haired Cambridge-Communist nonsense here."

So out of the club I went. I was not the first or last person to be ordered to leave by Colonel Gallagher. The procedure was simple. No matter how gross the insult he gave you, you apologized, not he. This drill being explained to me by the Stones, I was soon reinstated in the Colonel's good books. He was a nice old chap, really, and a year or two later he proved a real friend to me.

I used to have dusts-up with a man called Charles Abbot. We were good friends but, somehow, we always found ourselves taking opposite sides in any discussion—even if it meant contradicting ourselves to do so. The trouble was that we both wanted to talk at the same time. I found it easier to get

114

an audience than he because Abbot, poor fellow, wore people out before he got to the point. I would get to the point first, and then wear them down as they attempted to refute what I said.

Those of us among the English colony who were unmarried were expected to live at the Continental Hotel, a smart, cool, hygienic and luxurious place. I preferred to live in the back streets and try to learn modern Greek. Though I was paid about twenty pounds a month, living in those days was so cheap that I was able to stay at a good small hotel, belong to the Club, hire motor cars, and still have enough money to come home during the summer holiday. I settled in a hotel run by a Greek called Takkis, where I had a large room, laundry service, meals and a man to shave me, all for £7 10s. 0d. a month.

Things were livened up on one occasion by a visit from Osbert Sitwell and Tom Driberg. These two masters—in their different fields—of modern prose were passing through on their way to the Middle East.

My position, as a teacher of young Greeks, was not altogether a happy one. Despite my friends on the island, I was always regarded with suspicion and hostility by the pupils. It was, after all, only two or three years after the rather silly "rebellion" of 1931, when the Enosis movement, led by the bishops, burnt down Government House in Nicosia and the Commissioner's House in Limasol. As a result of this, the Legislative Assembly had been abolished and the Governor ruled by decree. There was still a rather disagreeable atmosphere of which, as has already been indicated by my brush with Colonel Gallagher, I was occasionally too critical.

I think it fair to say that the British Government had done its best for Cyprus. Unfortunately, the principles of fair play and impartial justice, which this country has always striven to maintain, were not always scrupulously observed by certain officials and native police officers. The sort of thing I disliked was that, under Government decree, *habeas corpus* was suspended as a result of the riots of 1931. The police had power to arrest anyone and keep him as long as they liked.

Naturally, the authorities were very sensitive about this and one was expected to keep one's mouth shut—a task I always found difficult.

One day I was being shown round a prison. Scores of scowling resentful Greeks squatted in the sunlit quad. I did not like the spectacle of these proud men in such a predicament and told the native guard to get me away.

"But you must see this prize Communist," the guard grinned, and led me to a corner where a young boy of about seventeen sat in the shade alone. He looked like a sculptured Greek god and there was a fineness about his features that belied the guard's statement.

"Hey, you!" shouted the guard, "stand up."

The boy ignored his command.

"Stand up!" shouted the guard, kicking the seated boy.

The boy refused to move.

"Leave him alone," I told the guard.

The boy looked up at me. Shame and nausea overwhelmed me. "Leave him, I say," I repeated.

Whether the boy understood what I was saying or not I shall never know. But as I was protesting with the guard he slowly got up and, staring into my face, spat directly at me.

This so infuriated the guard that he punched the boy violently.

"You should not have done that," I shouted angrily.

"What's the matter?" the man asked. "He's only a Communist."

Later, I discovered the boy's "crime." He had been caught with a stencilled Greek transcription of Shaw's *Intelligent Woman's Guide to Socialism*.

With great reluctance I ran a football team. The boys played very badly and always lost their tempers. One day a boy called Arde Anidras was involved in a fight on the pitch and was hauled off by watching policemen. That was the last I saw of him for some time. On enquiring what the police had done with him, I was told that he was being held in custody for creating a breach of the peace in a public place. I began to investigate the scandal.

"What is wrong with the boy?" I asked an official.

"He's a trouble maker."

"He wasn't making any trouble on the soccer pitch," I protested. "It was the others who ganged up on him."

"He created a breach of the peace."

"Rubbish," I said. "I shall get a lawyer to take up his case."

"I wouldn't, if I were you," the official said coolly.

"Why not?" I asked.

"You might find yourself in trouble. You don't want to be branded as a trouble maker, too, do you?"

That really angered me. I hate threats and innuendos. Briefing a lawyer, we went to court on the boy's behalf. Our defence was that the school's football pitch was not a public place. We won the case. This did not stop the police from having their revenge. They closed the football ground on the pretext that it was a meeting-place for agitators.

After a year at Limasol I took a long holiday and then went back to Cyprus to work in the Turkish Lycée at Nicosia. The chairman of my Board there was an amiable Turk called Munir Bey, who was very pro-British. Here I was much better off than at Limasol. I was provided with rooms at the Lycée, the Board going so far as to install a bathtub for me.

My routine was pleasant and simple. The boys were brighter and rather nicer than the Greeks in many ways. Some were, in fact, distinctly bright and intelligent, always a help in the harassing business of teaching. I had a comfortable time. Moslems never work on Friday. Since they did not expect me to work on Saturdays and Sundays, my working week began on Monday and ended on Thursday. Perhaps "working" is too strong a word for the gentle somnambulance of those days at Nicosia. To avoid the terrible midday heat lessons started at seven o'clock and finished at half-past eleven, when I would jog off to the English Club and drink pink gin. Then back to the school for a pleasant lunch of cheese and salad, washed down by the good wine of the island. Afterwards I went to bed to avoid the merciless temperature of the afternoon. In the cool of the evening I would rise and change and stroll back to the English Club for a weak whisky and soda, followed, in God's good time, by dinner and bridge.

I soon found that the Government was wrong in thinking that all Turks were pro-British while all Greeks were not. The influence of Kamal Ataturk was strong. The students did not wear military uniform, as my Greeks had done, but they did effect military caps. As the Greeks looked to Athens so my new charges looked to Ankara.

When, therefore, the authorities began planning celebrations for King George V's Jubilee, I was in the position to offer certain good advice. Rather stupidly, the Government ordained that all school children should sing "God Save the King" in their own language. Now Moslems cannot ask God to bless or save an infidel. To comply with the Government's decree, however, they were given translations of our National Anthem. The first line of this was: *Cok, cok Kiral*. When I discovered that my pupils were singing this as *Cok, cok Kamal* (Allah bless Kamal Ataturk) I warned the authorities to make them learn the English words. As is usual with well-intentioned advice, it was ignored. So when the great day dawned, the loyal anthem to good King George became an overwhelming hosannah in praise of the Turkish dictator!

I also remember that the Turks protested very strongly against the flying of the Union Jack. Their point was that, if there was to be any flag at all, it should be the flag of Turkey. This involved much petty bickering as flags were hauled up and down at the slightest whim: it was all very difficult and silly.

Highlight of the celebrations was the ceremonial visit of the Fleet. Admiral Sir Roger Backhouse came to Cyprus "wearing" (I believe that is the proper phrase) his broad pennant in *Revenge*. The usual exchange of visits took place. The ship's company were wined and dined ashore and then it was to be the Admiral's turn to invite the island's V.I.P.s to a dinner party aboard *Revenge*.

I was in a group talking to the Admiral ashore in the English Club. This included the island's Commissioner, the Harbour Master and Judge Green. When the time came for him to go back to the ship, the Admiral asked each one of us to dine with him the next day. I thought it somewhat odd that Judge Green was not included in the invitation, but assumed that he must have been asked earlier. "I'll send my barge," were the Admiral's parting words.

Duly attired in borrowed tails, I was piped on board the flagship. To my astonishment, the Admiral introduced me to the company as Judge Green.

"I am not Judge Green, sir," I said.

"Who the devil are you, then?" snapped the Admiral.

"Harding, sir."

"And what the devil do you do?"

"Teach English at the Turkish Lycée, sir."

"The devil you do. And what are you doing here?"

"You asked me to dinner, sir."

The Admiral stared thoughtfully at me.

"Oh, well," he said at last, "since you are here we had better make the best of it." We did. We had a very nice evening.

Soon after this I had to attend the funeral of the island's Archbishop. He was very old when he died and very fragile. The weather is so hot there that it is usual, when people die, to bury them at once. But not the Archbishop; he had to be kept for "proper burial." Richly dressed in his vestments and wearing his tall mitre and other symbols of episcopal office, he was to be buried seated in his chair.

It was very hot on the day when they at last got round to burying the old man. I took my place near the corpse, sitting directly behind the Governor's A.D.C., a young officer whose habitually red face and neck were complemented that day by the heavy scarlet tunic he wore for the occasion. The burial service seemed interminable. I felt curiously detached from it all as, from the tail of my eye, I alternately saw the blue mottled face of the bishop, dead in his chair, and the red bulging neck of the A.D.C. I think it was the smell of burning incense, to which I was accustomed, that saved me from succumbing to this prospect of death and decay. It had, however, the opposite effect on the youngster in front of me. Suddenly I saw this wretched boy's neck go pale, then green. I tapped him on the epaulette and took him out just in time. We found a cool bar and drank the funeral out there. No more elaborate funerals for me, I vowed, and I have avoided them like the plague ever since.

At Nicosia, I lived right in the heart of the old city, under the shadow of the Cathedral—now a mosque—of St. Sophia. I would time my day according to the comings and goings of the imam, or priest, going up into the minaret and calling the faithful to prayer. Many of my friends were Cypriots, but not all. There was, for instance, the head of the Forestry Department, a kindly old fellow whom I always enjoyed visiting for the pleasure and benefit of his good conversation. He had one violent prejudice, however—goats. There was in my time a ceaseless war between the forestry people and the peasants who depended on their goats for milk and meat. Now there is nothing goats like better than young trees, so the mere mention of these animals would upset him. "Don't talk to me about goats," he would fume, growing purple with anger. "They are devils! Fiends! They are sent by the devil to eat my trees!"

One day I showed him a photograph of a goat, taken during a Turkish feast, and told him that I was seriously thinking of having one as a pet. That really got his goat.

I did adopt a camel, once. I lived very near the bazaar and enjoyed wandering through the lovely narrow streets, watching the native tradesmen squatting in the shade, hammering copper, spreading out their wares, selling the island's rancid butter and figs and plums and raisins. Near my quarters was a great khan, or inn, where people used to put up their camels for the night. One day a boy told me that his camel had died, leaving a baby camel without a mother. I took the little creature back to my rooms and fed him on milk, and shared my food with him, till he got too big and smelly to have about the place.

There was also a baby donkey. I kept him under my roof for weeks, feeding him and giving him a little stall in the courtyard. When he needed exercise, I would take him gently by the ears and promenade him through the streets, talking to him as I would to any human friend. In the end, he too, had to go to carry tourists up the steep slopes to St. Hilarion.

Each morning when the barber came to shave me, I would be regaled with the latest gossip. It was very depressing. The people were desperately poor, the average income of the ordinary peasant being about twelve to fifteen pounds a year. So he would go off to the moneylenders and borrow up to sixty pounds which he could never hope to repay. Nearly all the rich merchants were moneylenders and nearly all the peasants had pledged their lives and belongings to some merciless extortioner. The really rich merchants found it convenient to live in Athens and have their blood-sucking done for them by agents.

The property laws were fantastic, and consequently there was a great passion for litigation. It was possible for a man to own the land but not the trees on it, while another might own the trees but not the fruit on them. Human life was held in small account. Each week would bring news of some new murder, often committed for some trivial reason, and the Government was gravely concerned over the number of death sentences which had to be passed.

Trial was not by jury but by three judges—a Puisne Judge, the President of the district court, and a Greek and Turkish Judge. Proceedings were all in English, with an interpreter in attendance. A good friend of mine at the time was a man called Bairamanian, an Armenian. This brilliant man was an official of the supreme court. Not only did he speak English as well as his native language, he was also master of Turkish, Greek, German and French—a one-man United Nations.

Sometimes I would be invited to dinner at Government House. This was always an amusingly formal and pompous proceeding. As representative of the British Monarch, the Governor, Sir Richmond Palmer, went into dinner first, was seated first and served first, attended by his Kavass, the Turkish bodyguard who accompany him everywhere, aloofly attentive in colourful baggy breeches and fez. At the end of the meal, the Governor was the first to leave the room; he and his lady did not go out, they "withdrew." They did not say good-night; the Governor's A.D.C. tactfully tipped the senior lady among the guests the wink when it was time to make herself scarce, and everyone else followed suit.

There was a good deal of fuss about precedence, Agriculture leaving before Public Works, and so on. Since I did not come under any Government category, I always found myself at the bottom of every list, the last to enter and the last to leave— not always a bad thing and certainly a curb on one's soaring ego.

A certain amount of lustre was added to my status after I became "Our Correspondent" for *The Times*. I was by now dickering with the idea of becoming a journalist and was glad of the opportunity of getting my foot wedged into the gateway to Fleet Street. I cannot have provided the venerable *Times* with any scoops, for about the only thing I seem to remember doing was to interview Jean Batten when she touched down at Cyprus on her way solo from Australia to England. I drove over the so-called airport (it was no more than a landing strip) and went through the usual fatuities of all such contrived and arbitrary interviews. I cannot remember what the flier said or what I wrote, but I rather feel that she reached London before my report reached Printing House Square.

One of my jobs on the island was to teach English to native policemen. At the end of the course there would be an examination by the board of examiners of which I was a member.

One day we were due to put a dozen or so policemen through their paces. It was terribly hot, so I suggested to my colleagues that we might shorten the proceedings by giving each candidate an oral examination instead of sweltering through the dreary business of paper work. They agreed, and I was asked to devise a test with the object of seeing how well the men understood English.

The first one came in, saluting smartly. Feeling very pleased with myself, I said: "Go out into the courtyard and collect six pebbles. Bring them in here and give one to me, put one on the mantelpiece, and give one to each of my four friends." Saluting smartly, he went to do as he was told.

After a while he came back and carried out my instructions perfectly.

"Thank you," I said blandly. "You can go now."

Another salute and he went.

"Well, gentlemen, what do you think?" I asked.

"Seems to be working very well," a colleague agreed.

"Very well, then," I said. "Now let us have the next one in. I'll ask the questions again if you don't mind."

So the second policeman was sent. He also saluted smartly and waited for instructions. To him I said: "Go to the bookcase behind you. Take one book out of the top shelf, two out of the middle shelf, and one from the bottom. Open the last book on page ninety-six and read what it says on the fifth line."

The man saluted smartly, turned on his heel and left the room, leaving the examiners to gaze in bewilderment at the shut door. After rather a long interval, the door opened again and our policeman re-entered, carrying six pebbles which he began to hand round. We decided that my brainwave would not do at all and in spite of the heat, went back to more orthodox methods of examination.

Shortly after all this I decided to return to England and try my luck in Fleet Street. I left the island in a terrible "tizzy." Some Russians who worked at Skouriotissa had promised to arrange a passage for me in a freighter, but when I got to the port I found that they had done nothing about it. By chance I heard of a berth going on another ship and this led to a wild dash across the island to Pathos where I caught the ship as it was about to cast off. Only when I got aboard did I realize that the ship was going in the other direction, to Port Said, at which delectable spot I had to hang about for several days until I got a passage on a Dutch boat.

Having been assured that this was a freighter, I was somewhat put out to find, when it docked, that it was a magnificent passenger boat. The first night I found my way into the saloon barred by an officious Dutch steward who informed me that I would have to go back to my cabin and dress for dinner. I told him not to be such an ass. A crowd began to collect round us as I continued to protest against this arbitrary ruling. (Besides which, I did not have a dinner jacket just then.) On being told for the tenth time that I would not be allowed into the saloon without a dinner jacket, I demanded to see the captain. On being taken into his presence, I pointed out that his contract of passage compelled him to give me victuals and drink but did not say when or where I was to eat them. They gave way and I spent the rest of the voyage to Southampton feeling as I imagine Aneurin Bevan might feel when attending a palace banquet wearing a lounge suit and red tie: bloody but unbowed.

"An assistant in the Outside Broadcasting Department."

Photograph: Angus McBean. Copyright: Home Companion

G.H. with Mother, to whom this book is dedicated.

The Brains Trust: Lord Samuel, Kingsley Martin, Bertrand Russell, G.H.

Round Britain Quiz: Jack House, G.H. and John Russell.

14

FLEET STREET, upon closer inspection, proved a less friendly place than I had imagined it to be from dipping into the writings of Sir Philip Gibbs. Aylmer Vallance might have given me a job on the *News Chronicle* if in the middle of our negotiations he and the owners of that paper had not parted company. I presented myself at *The Times* where nobody seemed at all interested in having their "Own Correspondent" from Cyprus so suddenly transported to their very doorstep. Harding in the abstract, it seemed, was a more attractive proposition than Harding in the flesh and in need of a staff job.

For a while I "stayed with people," that dreary genteelism which usually denotes the unwanted house guest eking things out with no visible means of support. It was not long before I began to get really fed up with having no money. It did not matter too much in Cyprus, but it did matter now. Soon I would be thirty years old and what had I to show in the way of material success? Precious little, I fear, and I did not enjoy the idea in any way.

One day I was dining with a rich stockbroker friend who had just received a hot tip. Halfway through the meal he was called to the telephone. He came back rubbing his hands, having made a lot of money, not only for himself but for two other guests. His wife, noticing how fed up I looked, said:

"Don't let's talk any more about money. You know how it only annoys Gilbert."

To which my friend replied: "Very well then. I shall make him some, too."

I smiled sourly. "Rot," I said. "You can't make money if you haven't any to start with in the first place."

"We shall see," said my host, and we changed the subject and went on with the meal.

A week or two later my friend sent me a cheque for well over £100 with a note saying. "It isn't as big as I thought it would be, but it's all yours."

I immediately rang him up. "But I can't possibly accept that money," I told him, feeling like Caesar and the crown.

"Don't you want it?" my friend asked.

"Of course I want it," I said, "but how on earth am I entitled to it?"

"That's simple," chuckled the stockbroker. "After dinner that night I lent you some money and followed up a hunch with it. The hunch came off, I've paid myself the money back, and the cheque I sent you is the gravy."

"You must have been barmy," I said, "to put your name to such a loan in the first place."

"Do you mean the original sum I lent you?" asked my friend.

"Yes."

"Oh, that's all right," said the stockbroker airily. "I didn't actually have to write out a cheque. It was all done over the telephone."

"So that's what is known as flying a kite?" I asked wonderingly.

"More or less. Goodbye."

"Wait," I said.

"Yes?"

"If I return this cheque you sent me, will you put the money on another hunch?"

"Certainly not," my friend said. "You can't be lucky all the time. Take my advice and keep well away from stockbrokers." I hurried round to my bank with my windfall wondering what to make of it all.

There was nothing for me to do but to teach again. So off I went to a small private school in a large and hideous country house near Longfield, Kent. The headmaster was a man

126

called Stickland and the place had room for about thirty boys who had failed for one reason or another to pass the necessary preliminaries before going to Woolwich, Sandhurst or the Royal Navy special entry examinations. There they were to be coached by Stickland and four assistants of whom I was one.

Two of us lived in. The other two, being married, lived out. I was quite comfortable, the work was not hard and the boys were not bad. (Far too many of them were killed in the war.) My opposite number among the masters was a man called Keef. It will give some idea of the tedium of our lives there when I say that the most exciting moments of each day were devoted to our joint onslaught on *The Times* crossword puzzle.

Keef and I made it a point to complete as much as we could before breakfast, each one concentrating on his own copy of the paper until it was time to sit down to that meal. Later we compared results and generally found that what one had not got the other had, and *vice versa*. In this Jack Sprat manner we usually managed to complete the crossword unaided by anyone else and without using dictionaries. Not my idea of fun, really.

The most pleasant time in that period of my life was when Keef and I made trips into the pleasanter parts of Kent. Keef was a great ordnance survey map man and knew every out-of-the-way acre of south-east England. We enjoyed each other's company and really found tremendous pleasure from such harmless diversions as retracing the old Pilgrim's Way to Canterbury, or crossing the coastal marshes without getting our boots wet.

After a term or two at Longfield, however, I began to make new plans. I had always wanted to go to the Bar and become a lawyer. Now the same gravitational pull which had drawn me so inevitably to the Bradford City Police Force began to exert its old power again. My grandfather had put me off when, as a schoolboy, I had once foolishly told him how nice it would be to study law. Taking me to London he led me to the Temple. Starting from the Strand we slowly made our way to the Embankment, looking at the names of the men who had chambers there. Then sitting down on a bench overlooking the Thames, my grandfather asked:

"How many names did you see?"

"Oh, hundreds," I said.

"How many have you ever heard of before?"

"Oh, about six," I said. "Patrick Hastings, Curtis Bennett, Horace Avory, Norman Birkett. Six or seven I reckon."

"And," said my grandfather impressively, "do you think you'll be another one in twenty years' time? Or will you be just one of hundreds grubbing around year after year for pettifogging briefs?"

It was a clumsy, brutal argument. But it succeeded in putting me off. I have since learnt that, when pressed to forecast exactly what I would become when I grew up, my grandfather would say: "A comedian. I can see no future for him except on the halls." No wonder he did his best to steer me away from this most learned of learned professions!

But I continued to hanker after a legal career. I loved, and still love, the pomp and ceremony of the assizes and the Old Bailey. I love the formalities and subtleties of jurisprudence. London's Inns of Court, Gray's and Lincoln's, the Inner and Middle Temples, attract me no less for the architecture than for the strange alchemy of atmosphere, suggesting timelessness and tradition, which they always invoke. I cannot walk through Lincoln's Inn Fields, with its square laid out by Inigo Jones, without seeing in my mind's eye, patterns of history, vigorous and native, which tend to be lost among the more contemporary neon signs and milk bars. These are the patterns which have filtered to us through the genius of Hogarth, Fielding and Dickens. Wandering among the seventeenth-century stones of Gray's Inn, or through the squares and courts built on the former property of the Knights Templar, I am always reminded of the first haunted, fog-enshrouded paragraphs of *Bleak House*, and almost expect to be confronted by the eccentric Miss Flyte or the sinister Mr. Tulkinghorn.

Nothing so romantic lay behind my present bid to study law. I was sick of schoolmastering. I could not get a job in Fleet Street. So I would, I told myself, become a lawyer and perhaps confound my grandfather after all. My old friend, Colonel Gallagher, of the English Club at Limasol, had married a Miss Macaskie. Her brother was Nicholas Macaskie, K.C., a Master of the Bench of Gray's Inn. Thanks to his kindness and generosity I became a member of the Honourable Society of Gray's Inn and I began to "eat my dinners."

I left Stickland without any regrets because even the most charming country walks through Kent can become a bore if you are young and restless. I knew that before he set up on his own, Stickland had worked with a man called Marcy who ran a crammer's in Chancery Lane. So I saw Marcy and asked him to give me a job, which he did at six pounds a week, enough for me to live on and pay for my own student's fees.

The next year or so was a very happy time. I persuaded my sister to give up her lodgings and share a flat with me at Twickenham. It was fun installing furniture of one's own, collecting a few little treasures, and really feeling that once you had shut the front door behind you it was really home. We moved in the day King Edward VIII abdicated. Most of the day I spent at Marcy's. The big room looked out over Chancery Lane. I was always furious when a street musician came along with a hurdy-gurdy to play the most banal, yet insidious melodies right under our window. Angrily I would lean out of the window and shoo him off, only to find the fellow there two or three hours later. My threats having failed to get rid of him, I would fling him a shilling and tell him to go elsewhere. That would keep him away for a while. Years afterwards I discovered that the boys had briefed the hurdy-gurdy man to annoy me. He did very well out of us. The boys would give him a shilling to come to Chancery Lane and I would then give him a shilling to go away. An excellent arrangement for all except one harassed and not too even-tempered tutor.

I would teach from a textbook written by a man called Marcy. It was remarkable for the clever way in which it condensed the whole of English History into one slim volume, history being the subject for which I was cramming the boys. Marcy's book is the most wonderful précis I have ever seen, and I strongly recommend it to all aspirant history tutors. I still have my copy somewhere.

There I was, earning my living on one side of Chancery Lane and going to law lectures, whenever I could, on the other side. I was a diligent pupil in the Temple, passing my exams with surprising ease. Roman Law, Constitutional Law, Contract and Tort—all came easily to me.

My sister and I had furnished the flat on the hire-purchase system. We both had regular jobs and for me (perhaps spurred by her good example) it was early to bed and up at four for three hours' swotting before leaving for Chancery Lane. There always seemed to be enough money, and while we lived modestly, I was able, whenever I wanted, to see the latest plays, buy the books I needed, and eat in good restaurants. Working to a budget, we knew where we were and did not step over the limit.

The glorious spring of the year that followed my return to this country burst into the high summer of the King's happy Coronation. It was good to be in London and share the mounting excitement and mysteriously communicated sense of community which spasmodically erupts in our national character, to become something quick and alive and then heavy with spiritual undertones. Looking back, it was, I suppose, an unconscious girding up of the loins in preparation for the ugly afflictions that lurked ahead. One experienced a similar sense of communal joy and unconscious dedication during the crowning of our present Queen. I pray that no worse national endurance tests await us, as they did in that strangely tranquil summer of 1937 when anyone with ears to hear could not ignore the mutterings and explosions in Germany, Italy, Spain.

Near our flat was a very nice pub, the Cole Court Hotel, now unhappily a Free Masonic temple. There I would occasionally go to relax after an excess of study. The Twickenham studios were busy then, and I would find the hotel full of film people. They were usually very nice and I used to envy them a great deal, but not too much, as they prattled over their pink gins and Pimms. There was a very pleasant script writer called Barringer, while Julius Hagen, owner of the studios, was always approachable. That fine, dependable actor, Garry Marsh, was also a stalwart at the Cole Court bar and I found myself vaguely wanting to take a more active share in this life of shadow-projection and personality play. Then I would sternly remind myself that I was a serious student of jurisprudence, and return to my books and my dawn studies.

The Coronation year of George VI passed into the next, a year when the war trumpets began to sound more insistently and the world crisis became as much part of the household prattle as the word cricket. For me, however, they were years of real hard work. I was determined that my boys should not fail their examinations, and few did. For my part, I wanted to pass the Bar examinations, and there was every hope of my doing so. I was, then, not without incentives, and the fact that I had only sufficient money on which to live comfortably, but without excess, curbed any tendencies I might have had to show off or indulge myself unduly.

I remember an amusing incident about this time which well illustrates the appalling, but not altogether unreasonable snobbishness of our social structure. We had in my class a boy—call him Vincent—who had everything in the way of mental and physical equipment to fit him for a commission in the Army. He only came to us because he would undoubtedly pass the Civil Service Commission (Army Entrance) but hoped, by diligent cramming, to get even higher marks. Vincent was, however, handicapped by a very bad cockney accent, of which he was happily at that time unaware. It was not my place to point it out, however. To the best of my recollection, out of 1,000 total marks for the examination with which this brilliant boy was concerned, 250 were for "interview and record," in other words, oral examination. For the written part of his examination, Vincent actually did achieve the exceptionally good total of 600 marks, but in "interview and record" he flopped badly enough to put him far enough down the list to fail.

Vincent's father was horrified. One afternoon he called on me and asked what had gone wrong. I told him. "But," said he, a fine militant cockney himself, "you can't penalize a kid just for the way he talks."

"Unfortunately," I said, "you can. I won't pretend to approve of such discrimination, but it exists and the only thing to do about it is fight it on its own terms."

"How can we do that?" asked the father.

"Send him to an expert elocution master," I said. The father was well off enough to do this. The second time Vincent took the examination he spoke with sufficient "lah-de-dah" to achieve a good place in the examination—just in time to get killed in the war.

About this time I met a number of B.B.C. people and there was some vague talk of my applying for a job, but it never amounted to much.

By the summer of 1939—refusing to admit to myself that there ever could be a war, and having saved enough on which to live for six months—I decided to stop working for a living and concentrate on passing the Bar finals. Having found a barrister friend to take me as a pupil for nothing instead of the usual hundred guineas, I went to work on an all-out concentrated assault on becoming a lawyer.

Everyone knows what happened on September 3, 1939. On that day, after hearing Mr. Chamberlain's saddened and disillusioned statement that a state of war existed between this country and Germany, I closed my book on equity and have never opened a law book since.

My first move was to visit my mother at Bradford. There was little enough to say in the light of the vast tragedy which was tearing up families all over Europe. I seem to have spent much of my time helping Mother get up the blackout curtains all over the hospital. These tasks over, I felt, as usual, in the way. My mother was so busy, and I simply could not follow her around with medicine bottles and bandages. I managed to get a temporary job as a clerk in the office of the Registrar of Births, Deaths and Marriages in the City of Bradford. I learnt how to issue copies of certificates concerning these acts of human mortality and how to consult files and records. It was dull work and left me baffled and frustrated at the end of each day.

At that time you had to have influence to get into the Army at all. Medically I had not got certificate "A" and I had one very good reason for not going into the ranks. Having earned my living for years being violently offensive and sarcastic to young men who I knew would now be captains and majors only too glad to get their own back, I decided that it would have to be a commission or nothing. For a while I was faced with the prospect of nothing—a depressing situation for anyone.

Nothing seemed to be happening in the war. A good time was being had by all jacks-in-office and jumped-up local officials. Apart from that, our noble crusade did not seem to amount to much. The great lion, Churchill, had not begun to growl. I was thirty-two and not due for call-up for some time, so I got another crammer's job, this time at the University Tutorial College in Red Lion Square, London. I cannot say that I was overjoyed to be back to teaching.

I had not been in London long when one morning there came a telegram saying, "If interested in post Overseas Service please contact me at B.B.C. signed Salt." At last the B.B.C. were inviting me to join their staff. I looked at the

133

telegram in my hand, conscious—as I had been when I heard the news from Cyprus—that this piece of paper would effect infinite changes in my life, changes unforeseen and unpredictable. It was the first time I came across the horrible verb "contact," but even as my schoolmaster's mind deplored its use, my restless and curious spirit was projecting me swiftly and alarmingly forward. Within ninety minutes of receiving the telegram at Twickenham I was at Broadcasting House.

I went to see a man called Ambler, a charming fellow who is now dead. As General Establishment Officer it was his business to tell me how much I was to be paid.

"Your starting salary will be £480 a year," he said.

"But that's wonderful," I exclaimed.

"What!" said he, "do you mean to say you think it's enough?"

"Enough, my dear fellow?" I replied. "I think it's marvellous."

He stared at me in amazement. "Do you know," he said, "that's the first time anyone has said that to me. Let's go and have a drink."

That was how my first B.B.C. job—with the Monitoring Service—began: over a large Scotch.

15

THE Second World War was still at its "phoney" stage when I started work on the second floor of Broadcasting House. I was now getting more money than I had ever earned before and I settled down to it with a will, determined to make a worthwhile career with the B.B.C.

It was a curious job and went something like this. The B.B.C. had set up a listening service in the country (at Evesham, but that was very hush-hush then) where, in considerable discomfort and under cloak-and-dagger supervision, people of all nationalities listened to foreign broadcasts in practically every language. These would be translated into English and sent by teleprinter to London, where people like me would be employed as sub-editors to make a "daily digest of foreign broadcasts."

Most of my colleagues had been recruited from Fleet Street. I covered up the fact that I lacked any kind of inside journalistic experience by listening eagerly and assiduously to those who had. But I must have had something because before you could say Jack Robinson I was chief sub-editor. (That meant another £120 a year.) Then before you could say another Jack Robinson, I was an "Information Bureau Supervisor." All the teletypes came to us first, and it was our business to skim them for "flashes" and tell the various Service departments about anything of immediate interest. Some sentences were scrambled, some messages were printed in various colours, and a glorious kind of Phillips Oppenheim mystery atmosphere prevailed.

One incident I shall never forget. Late one night a voice came over one of the signal lines to inform me that the First Lord of the Admiralty wanted to speak to me. I waited and a few seconds later the famous voice of Winston Churchill asked:

"Is there anything important from Norway?"

"Norway?" I repeated. "No, sir. Not yet."

"Please to keep me informed on this line," Churchill said.

"Yes, sir."

It was not long before the Norwegian radio began to complain of mining of their territorial waters by the British Navy. I quickly got a line to Churchill and thus it was that the war leader learned that the war was beginning in earnest. Bombs became a nightly accompaniment to London life, and Broadcasting House became a humming fortress of communication. The Monitoring Service did wonderful work. By that time the reception engineers had reached such a degree of perfection that they were able to pick up inter-aircraft communications between German pilots. In a matter of minutes we could warn the R.A.F. of the Nazi fliers' intentions. Enemy bombers were frequently intercepted and driven back as a result of stray German intercom. messages picked up by our service.

My most spectacular recollection of this was finding myself listening to two Focke-Wulfe pilots exulting over the shooting down of a Sunderland Flying Boat off the East Coast. Within a few minutes of our hearing this, an air-sea rescue launch was on its way from Felixstowe to pick up the pilots who had been shot down.

On the lighter side, I remember the special alarm under my desk, controlled by a lever near my feet. In the event of an invasion I was supposed to press this to set off an elaborate sequence of security measures. One day I absent-mindedly touched the lever with my foot. Immediately iron doors clanged to throughout the building, bells rang, and a contingent of Home Guards rushed in at the double. It did not help much when I apologetically explained that I had just been stretching my legs.

My crazy days at Broadcasting House came to an end and I was precipitated into the even crazier atmosphere of Evesham, where we worked night and day in the oddest circumstances. Everyone there had become cloak-and-dagger minded and sometimes this was carried to extremes. We were protected by the Army, a tedious business which entailed showing one's pass every few yards. With hundreds more, I was billetted on the long-suffering inhabitants of that peaceful country town. Long before I arrived these good people had had more than their share of shocks. When the Drama Department moved in, for instance, the town was inundated with young persons of either or doubtful sex, carrying Siamese cats and teddy bears.

There we were, the rag-tag and bobtail of the arts, of journalism and academic life, flung upon this quiet agricultural community with a sprinkling of sad and weary displaced persons from the Continent, long exiled from their homelands and at last employed to listen and record the story of their country's ruin. The whole place was a miasma of human misery and degradation. The exacting work, the long hours and the dreary night shifts, gave each face a grey and sallow aspect that reminded one of the shuffling ghosts in Dante's spiralled hell. The frightful stupidity of the military guards and special police, who seemed to regard intellectuals, Jews and foreigners as scum, made for every kind of short temper. Nerves were strained and every one was just on the edge of breaking point.

Long and scarcely audible telephone conversations made for madness. All the ballyhoo and claptrap of unimportant little men dressed in a little proud brief authority came to the surface and made life a hell for anyone in their power. We worked in huts inadequately separated by shoddy wooden partitions. We were so accustomed to being challenged by sentries that we did not resent showing our passes even when we strolled from our cubby holes to the lavatories. The same futile, time-wasting, temper-fraying procedure would hold up our progress between our offices and the canteen.

The canteen was housed in the mansion of Wood Norton, built by the Duke of Orleans. At the entrance from the Pershore Road stood the Golden Gates, ornately gilded to befit the house of Orleans. One evening, as I was going on duty, I found my way barred by a sloppily dressed soldier, whose business it was to check my identity card. Though I had little time to spare, this young lout apparently thought I had an eternity in which to wait while he dallied with a kitchen maid.

"Oo, go on, George," giggled the girl. "You know I can't see you tomorrer night."

"Aw, 'course you can, Lil," replied the sentry.

"Can't."

"Can."

"Can't, I tell yew."

"Go on, be a sport, Lil."

"But I can't, George. Hon'st."

"You're lying."

"I'm not."

"Yes, yew are."

"No, I'm not."

This fascinating exchange might have continued till the end of the war had I not suddenly caught the sentry by his arm and wheeled him round to face me.

"Now," I said sternly, "you are going to examine this pass and let me go about my business. But before you do this, let me point out that you have committed at least three breaches of King's Regulations. You have failed to dress properly. You have neglected your duty. You have made romantic overtures to a civilian whilst on duty. So smarten up and let me get the hell through."

Sullenly the boy buttoned his greatcoat and, avoiding the girl's eyes took my pass and examined it. Then he handed it back without a word, merely nodding for me to proceed.

"Coo, he's a stuck-up high-and-mighty so-and-so," I heard the girl say as I went up the drive.

"Aw, forget him," said the sentry. "He can count hisself lucky. I wouldn't have taken that from one of them Jew foreigners."

This sullen spirit infested the whole place, yet much work was done. Lots of programmes originated from Evesham, and there were occasional moments of light relief. One day a woman arrived at the Golden Gates in a taxi and asked to be let through. When asked to produce her pass she rummaged in her bag and said she had lost it. The sentry refused to let her in.

"But you must let me in," said the woman. "I'm Madame Stella and I am broadcasting in a few minutes."

"I'll ring the controller," said the sentry and went to the telephone.

Now the taxi driver decided to liven matters up. "Sorry, lady," he said. "Afraid you'll have to pay me off now. I've got to meet a train and I'm late already."

"But you can't leave me here with my instrument."

"Sorry, lady."

"Oh, very well, give me a hand with it to the gate." Out of the taxi stepped Madame Stella and, with the driver's help, dragged out an enormous harp.

The sentry looked up in surprise just as he got through to the controller.

"Sorry to bother you, sir," he said, "but Madame Stella is at the Golden Gates with her harp."

"All right," said the Controller. "Tell her the angels won't keep her long."

Winston Churchill again touched my life. At Evesham I was on a kind of marathon night shift which always began at 2 a.m. I had, by the way, been promoted again, and my salary was now £840 a year. My main duty was to deal with what was called the Cabinet Report. The monitors who listened twenty-four hours a day recorded and reported their material. This was then sub-edited and edited and duplicated and then given to one of four people for final "break-down" for transmission to the War Cabinet in London. I was one of the four, and frequently relayed the day's report direct to Churchill. I learnt that, when I was off for two weeks, the Prime Minister asked for me, saying: "Where is that man with the succinct mind?"

Though I was now "sitting pretty" and holding down a "cushy job," I could not settle at Evesham. Night after night I was moved, sometimes to anger, sometimes to pity, by the staff of underpaid, badly housed, atrociously fed women whose business it was to cut the stencils and type. They were under the control of overseers and for as little as £2 15s. 0d. a week were on duty all night. The huts in which they worked were either too hot or too cold and were always badly ventilated. Like us, the movements of these girls were constantly checked by sentries and their privacy was negligible. It became a wry joke among them to say: "If there is a fire, we'll send for a fireman—and hope to God that he hasn't forgotten his pass."

My habit of butting in when some petty official tried to devise a new humiliation for these overworked women did not make me one of the most popular people around the place. On one occasion I was highly infuriated when a smart Alec, from the safety of his executive's desk, began to berate a tired but enormously dignified Central European professor.

"Where did you get this information," I heard the man say as I entered his office. "What is the source?"

"But I have told you," the professor said patiently. "It is the latest policy line from the Wilhelmstrasse."

"The Wilhelmstrasse?" this erudite executive asked. "What the blazes is that?"

"The Wilhelmstrasse is the Berlin equivalent of Whitehall," the professor explained.

"Then why the heck don't you damn well say so," shouted the man at the desk. "You foreigners are all alike. Damned shifty lot who won't say what they mean."

I could no longer restrain myself. "All right, professor," I said, "I will explain to this man who, I am ashamed to say, is a fellow-Englishman."

There was a terrible row during which, naturally, I told

140

the fellow exactly what I thought of bullying pipsqueaks who insult people who are not in a position to fight back. Thus I added yet one more to my collection of people who have disliked me for speaking up instead of whining behind their backs.

As the war got more and more serious I longed to take a more active part. Lord Kennet's Committee investigating the call-up decided that the age should be raised. That made me available for National Service, but the doctors at Worcester rejected me *in toto* and that put an end to my conscience-stricken broodings about military life.

Sometimes I would go to London to check whether my flat at Twickenham was still in existence and to see my sister, Constance, who as a war-time school teacher was sorely overworked. Each time I came to London I discovered more gaps where once had stood landmarks of my pre-war life. Fortunately, several restaurants remained where it was possible to get a good meal and rehabilitate oneself after weeks of canteen fare. While sitting in one of these with several other B.B.C. men I mentioned that I was restless and hankering for more active work.

Though my work at Evesham was chiefly concerned with monitoring, I made my first broadcast from there.

It was in a series called "Voice of the Nazi." This was done each week by a Scottish professor. When he was unable to find the time I deputized for him. Being for the Overseas Service and therefore pre-recorded, I was able to hear my voice for the first time. It gave me an awful shock. Now, of course, I am used to it, but that first time—as happens to everyone—it was hard to realize that this detached voice was mine, as other people hear it. Still, I was not put off and shortly after I had aired my views in that London restaurant I was asked by Michael Standing, Director of Outside Broadcasts, to join his department.

Now an assistant in the Outside Broadcasting Department, I shared an office at Cavendish Square with Raymond Glendenning, Wynford Vaughan Thomas and Stewart MacPherson as colleagues. I soon found that I had a great deal to learn. Lots of things one took for granted turned out not so easy as they seemed. Though my first interview seemed the easiest thing in the world, it was never used for broadcasting. When it was played back it turned out to be an elaborate monologue by me with the interviewee occasionally saying, "Yes, that's right." I had committed the gross error of putting all the words in the wrong mouth.

I settled down at last and a regular weekly programme broadcast to America, called *Meet John Londoner*, became a terrible chore. I dreaded Tuesday, when we attended "briefing meetings" to be told which subjects to emphasize and which to avoid. Then out we would go into the streets with a recording car to find our people. When we had settled on one, the following exasperating rigmarole would be gone through.

The people were obviously more interested in us, and what we were doing, than in themselves.

"How does the mike work?" a lorry driver would ask. We would explain.

"Shall I be able to hear it?"

We would tell him no, the broadcast was for America.

"When does it go out to listeners?"

We were never sure.

"Do you know so-and-so whose brother's nephew is at the B.B.C.?"

We seldom did.

"Pity. He's a very clever bloke. Well educated."

"Now," we would ask, "are you ready to record a short interview with us?"

"No thanks, mate. I must be getting along."

We would have to find somebody else and, as likely as not, the whole thing would happen all over again.

On one occasion MacPherson and I were in Trafalgar Square. Mrs. Roosevelt was in London and it was our job to make this one of the points of discussion. After one or two shocks and disappointments we found a man who could have been sent from a casting agency with his script written for him by Robert E. Sherwood. He had just the right touch of the authentic cockney but not so much as to make him incomprehensible to Americans. He had a son in the Navy, another in the Air Force, his wife was a prominent worker in the W.V.S. and his two daughters were in the A.T.S. He himself, a retired N.C.O., was in the Home Guard. An ideal choice.

At the end of the interview, which went very well, Mac-Pherson said: "What do you think of Mrs. Roosevelt's visit to this country?"

"We are proud and honoured to have her here," said our jewel, "and to welcome her, and through her, her wonderful husband. All I hope is that the President himself can come some time so that we Londoners can cheer him in the streets and show him how much we all admire him."

This was magnificent stuff. Then I had to ask: "Have you seen Mrs. Roosevelt since she has been in London?"

"No," said our friend, "but I understand that her chief purpose in coming here is to have intercourse with the American troops."

There were other series in which I got interested. One was my own, called *The Mike Wants To Know*. This enabled me to do short documentary radio features on aircraft, destroyers, submarines, battle training schools, and a score of other things connected with the war effort. I learnt a lot in that department because Michael Standing, now Controller of Entertainment, had the excellent habit of listening carefully to everything that his assistants did and then quite often playing back the recordings to them, stopping every now and then for comments, favourable or unfavourable. Though he did not lightly hand out bouquets, at least one felt that someone cared.

In 1944, after two years of this outside broadcasting, I successfully applied for the newly created job of Assistant to the B.B.C.'s Canadian Representative in Toronto. I went off to Canada for the second time with the usual last-minute rush, complicated by silly wartime hush-hush regulations. I was not told the port of embarkation or on which ship I would be travelling and by the time I was ready to go I was in a foul temper. Checking this for a while, because my mother was coming to see me off, I drove to Euston Station in the middle of an air raid. Shortly before the train was due to leave, Mother looked at my wrist watch and said: "That reminds me. My watch is broken. Let me have yours in exchange for this." Whereupon she produced from her hand-bag a massive gold "turnip" which had belonged to my grandfather.

Hurriedly removing the wrist watch I made the swap as the train started to move. Shortly before my return to this country there was an amusing sequel to this, which I shall tell in its proper place. The train was hot and crowded and dirty and took ages to get us to our destination which turned out to be "somewhere in Scotland" and the following evening I sailed from Greenock in the old *Aquitania*.

16

THE voyage was quite unbelievably horrible. The ship was under contract to the United States Government. The service was nil, and the bar "dry." I soon finished off the bottle of whisky I had brought along on the trip and was served practically incessantly with Coca-Cola, not a drop of which I have touched since. Eight of us shared a cabin in which I am glad I had no cat, for there was certainly no room for swinging it.

The old liner was now a troopship carrying officers back from European service. It also carried the first batch of war brides. They were well looked after by the Canadian Red Cross, but this did not prevent them from making our days and nights hideous with their groanings and retchings as the ship heaved and tossed in the open sea.

Many of the mothers were pregnant: many more were carrying nursing babies in their arms. The squalls of angry babies and the screechings of massed motherhood made me thankful, not for the first time, that I was still a bachelor and more than likely to remain one for the rest of my life.

One of the nurses told me that she was afraid that some of these girls were in for a bit of a shock. A young bride going to join her husband in Winnipeg (where the nurse came from) showed her a photograph of her "new home." The nurse hadn't the heart to tell her that it was a photo of the Parliament Building.

We were not allowed to smoke on deck after dark and the constant boat drill was an unpleasant reminder that the sea around us was thick with submarines. I was very glad indeed to get to Halifax. There another setback confronted me. The immigration officials had not been told that I was coming and would not allow me to land. The B.B.C. had not taken the trouble to tell the authorities that I did not intend to earn money in Canada other than from official British funds. So angry was I with the stupid Bumbledom of the gum-chewing officials at Halifax that I almost went back. After a day's delay the difficulty was overcome and I set off to Montreal. So shocking is the railway service that this journey now takes eleven hours longer than it did when the railway was opened in 1867. Nor was I allowed to settle down to enjoy this trip. A war bride and her crippled soldier husband failed to get a berth on the train, so I gave up my own comfortable quarters and sat it out mostly in the observation car.

I arrived in Montreal cross and tired, a state from which I rarely seemed to recover during the rest of my stay in Canada. After a few weeks all my old irritations with North American life returned: annoyance at the liquor laws, which are even more fantastic than our own; contempt for provincial small-time snobberies; loathing for the food. Wherever I went I was given great lumps of half-cooked meat, with more for a helping than would meet the weekly ration in England. You were never passed a dish of butter without finding cigarette ash all over it. Coming from poorly rationed Britain I could not keep quiet when I saw pernicious examples of waste everywhere.

I think North American cooking is quite the worst in the world and I am convinced that Canadian and American hotels employ special officials to see that food is never served on a hot plate and that the staff is as rude as possible. Then there is the horrible habit of serving coleslaw and mountains of mayonnaise. It is quite useless to ask not to be given it. You'll get it whether you like it or not—even with kippers.

For a country which literally has everything Canada is the most backward—gastronomically—in the world. The people have some horrible eating manners. Catsup is liberally poured over everything: fish, beef, eggs. Ice cold milk is the favourite tipple. When you come to the pudding—the sweet as they call it—you are given tasteless frozen bits of cream and canned

146

fruit. At the end of a meal the waiter comes up to you and genially asks: "What's your bev?" This means, do you want tea or coffee. Tea is made with hot (never boiling) water strained through a little bag of poor quality tea.

Maddened by all this, you cannot seek the civilized alternative of ordering yourself a stiff drink. The results of the liquor laws lie like a heavy pall on Canada. When I got there in 1944 there had been no improvement on the absurdities which I described earlier. Naturally, half a bottle of whisky, gin or rum is not nearly enough for a month's supply, so it was always expedient to employ a teetotal secretary and use her liquor permit to augment yours. If you cannot get a liquor permit, then my advice is, get out of Canada just as fast as you can hoof it.

Culturally, Canada stinks. An impresario took Toscanini to the liquor store to get a permit.

"Occupation?" demanded the clerk.

"Conductor," said Toscanini, and on the permit was written T.T.C.—Toronto Tramways Commission.

I had not travelled much in Canada in the 1930's: this time I went far afield. The country still allowed itself to be called a Dominion, and there was a fine spirit of community between itinerant Englishmen like myself and residents. The country itself was stark and vast, and as my work took me ever farther afield, I enjoyed the sense of space and massive grandeur that is its strength and charm. Once again I fell under the magic spell of the Province of Quebec and particularly the glorious city on its great road above the mighty river. I never failed to enjoy the simple, refreshing courtesy of the French Canadians and the uprightness of the children. It was good to move around and watch the seasons blend and move across the vast canvas of the North American sky, to watch in autumn the big trees change colour and feel the flurry of fine snow against your cheeks as you moved through the dry winter air.

Once again I was thrilled by Montreal and revolted by

Ottawa. When I went to the West Coast I realized the amount of admiration due to the Canadians for having made so much out of such uncompromising material—those endless prairies and bare rocky mountains. I wish I had gone no farther than Calgary, that beautiful city on the foothills of the Rockies, where you find the very essence of North America at its best and its people make you think of the Mounties and *Rose Marie* and cowboys.

Alas, on the other side is Vancouver, and Victoria on Vancouver Island; and that you can have! Here they are more English than the English. I always found it most irritating to be told: "How I love your English accent." It was useless for me to protest that I had not got one. "How can I speak English with an English accent?" I would ask. "I might speak French or German with an English accent, but I just *speak* English. Anyhow, what is wrong with a Canadian accent?"

Etiquette was a fetish in Vancouver. Based on some Victorian never-never land of their own fantastic devising, there was an atmosphere that hovered crazily between Kipling's bullet-biting pukkah sahibs and the chorus of the Gaiety at the turn of the century. A friend of mine, whose sense of humour saved him from living in this fossilized way, asked me to stay with him and his delightful wife on Vancouver Island. Soon after they had married, their neighbours and friends had made them welcome by giving them a "shower," which is a nice North American custom of present-giving when young couples set up their own households. All brought something that would be useful in the home: saucepans, kettles, china, an electric iron, and so on. All, that is, except a certain major who never spoke to anyone unless he had been properly introduced. In a dinner jacket and straw hat with his Regimental colours on the band, he used to tend his roses in the garden a few yards from my friends' home, never speaking to them because they had not been introduced by an acceptable third party.

One day my friend's wife had a baby and her parents in England announced this in *The Times*. In due course, copies

148

reached Vancouver. On picking up his copy, the major read the announcement of a birth about which everybody in the neighbourhood knew, and the obvious manifestation of which was lying in a perambulator not far from where the major was sitting. Carefully scrutinizing this information which had travelled some three thousand miles across North America and another two thousand miles across the sea to London and back again, the major walked over and said: "Ah, I see you have a baby. Congratulations. I had no idea that your wife was a 'Whatnot-Wizzbang'."

I found Canada torn by a great conscription crisis and tempers ran high between the Canadians and the French Canadians. It was fashionable to detest MacKenzie King and adore Churchill, and I witnessed some spectacular quarrels.

The absurdity of racial prejudices was most amusingly illustrated for me one day in Toronto. I was crossing Jarvis Street from the Canadian Broadcasting Company's head-quarters building in company with a French-speaking Canadian, who was going to collect his laundry from a Chinaman called Fred Foo. Across his arm he had a pair of trousers. Having collected his laundry, he was paying for it when Foo said:

"Where you taking them pants?"

"Down to Issy's," said my friend, referring to an Austrian Jewish refugee who pressed clothes in a little shop down the road.

"You no want to go him," said the Chinese. "He's a goddam Jew."

"What the hell has that got to do with you?" said the Canadian. "You are only a Chink yourself."

Foo gave him a look of supreme contempt and said to me: "Lousy French Canadian."

I did not say anything.

"Say, what's biting you?" sneered the Chinese. "You've no right to criticize. You're only a stinking Limey, anyway."

What better example of racial and religious bias than this!

Jarvis Street, by the way, was the brothel street of Toronto. Having found comfortable rooms there, I moved in and was not in the least put off by my lurid neighbours. One evening I was at a dinner party when a pompous woman turned to me and asked:

"Well, and where do you live?"

"Jarvis Street," I said.

The woman looked disapprovingly at me.

"That's not a very fashionable address," she said superciliously.

"Neither is Toronto, madam," I replied, tucking into my steak.

At another function I was placed next to yet another female pillar of Toronto Society.

"What do you think of Canada?" she asked as an opening gambit.

"Marvellous," I replied, knowing the drill.

"Do you like Canadian art?"

"I think it is wonderful."

"And have you seen Niagara Falls?"

"Yes."

"What did you think of them?"

"Magnificent. Glorious. Marvellous. Wonderful."

If she had only been content with this and turned to the man at her other side all might have been well. But things were not destined to go smoothly.

"What do you think of the Conscription issue?" she went on.

"I think its opponents have a lot in their favour," I said.

"Really?" said my neighbour icily. "I don't. By the way, isn't it disgraceful the number of Catholics who are working for the B.B.C."

"No, it isn't," I said. "I happen to be a Catholic and I work for the B.B.C."

"At least I am sure you will agree with me that the French

Canadians are making an awful nuisance of themselves?"

"Not at all," I said. "I think they are a wonderful people and far more courteous than most of us."

"Come," snapped my neighbour. "I am broadminded but I think you are carrying things a little too far."

"I don't think I am," I replied. "I am merely answering your questions with as much honesty and patience as I can possibly contrive. I am not pro-Conscription. I am not anti-Catholic and I am certainly not against the French Canadians. I am not, in fact, against anything or anyone except crass stupidity. For my part I would be willing to employ, or work beside, not only French Canadians but Hindus, Kaffirs, Chinese, Rumanian Jews and Kentucky Minstrels."

"This is outrageous," the woman said, rising. "I refuse to sit here and be insulted. Stand up, sir."

"Why?" I asked. "I am perfectly comfortable as I am."

"Either you stand up and leave this table or I do."

"Well, I'm staying," I said. "I have no intention of being discourteous to my hosts."

So the woman flounced out and that is the last I ever saw of her.

Some of the finest people I ever met in Canada were the North American Indians. Once I had to go along and make a recording of a native rite called the Dance of the Green Corn. Obsessed as I was with technical problems, I could not help being carried away by the beauty and fierce joy of this strange dance. The music of the drums and the at first slow movements of the dancers rose to wild crescendos. Here, I felt, was the old blood of Canada resurging under a bright new moon. Strange gods seemed to lurk in the shadows as the Indians danced into the night by a flickering camp fire.

The fashionable thing, of course, was to look down on these people, rather as many of us in Britain tend to patronize gypsies. A genial lawyer in Vancouver once introduced me to a member of the Siwash Tribe. Before so doing he had dug me in the ribs and with a wink told me to listen carefully to what the Redskin said. It was bound to be good for a few laughs, he assured me.

"This guy, August Jack, is just one long scream from beginning to end," the lawyer said, roaring with laughter at the prospect of the fun we would have.

In fact, I found the Indian a tall, impressive man with the nobility of face and great dignity of the dispossessed. The lawyer asked August Jack to tell me the legend of the Siwash Rock which stands at the entrance of Vancouver Bay.

"This is a real scream," he added to me *sotto voce*.

Jack then told me the simple and pious legend of the Indian who went every morning to stand in the water and greet the Great Light of the Sun. Again in the evening he would go there and thank the Great Spirit for the happiness of the day and to wait for the Lesser Light of the Moon. Touched by the piety of this Indian, the Great Spirit rewarded him (Jack said) by turning him into a rock so he could stay in his beloved bay for ever. I thought this was a charming story and much more acceptable than a good many Christian legends. Not so my lawyer friend, who roared with laughter and said to me:

"Isn't that great?"

To the Indian he said: "You don't really believe that muck, do you, Jack?"

"Well, sir," said Jack, "I do."

"You don't mean it!" exclaimed my friend, between fits of laughter. "You can't possibly believe it."

"Do you believe in the Bible, sir?" Jack asked quietly.

"Course I do."

"You believe everything in it?"

"Why, sure, but this is different."

"O.K." said Jack. "What about Lot's wife? You can't show me that pillar of salt, but by jumping Jehoshaphat, there's that rock down there in the bay."

I thought that was definitely Jack's round, and told him so to the great annoyance of the lawyer.

Some weeks before Christmas, I found myself involved in the B.B.C.'s annual radio epic, the Christmas Day Hook-Up, which takes place during the hour which precedes the reigning monarch's speech at three o'clock. Now I know how much work Laurence Gilliam must put into this on the whole unrewarding job and as early as June we were asked to make suggestions for the best way to represent Canada. Was it to be a lumberjack talking from British Columbia? Or a miner from North Ontario? Or a Red Indian from one of the reserves? Or just a farmer on the prairie?

Offers and counter offers, suggestions and counter suggestions flashed to and fro between London and Canada. In the end it was decided there should be four minutes from a holiday hotel in the Laurentian Mountains above Quebec. There we went, moving into the place several days before the broadcast to select, coach and rehearse our subjects. We put the hotel staff to every known inconvenience. We chased guests out of their rooms in order to test the best possible locations. Though he knew that we would not be allowed to mention the name of his hotel, the proprietor, a cheerful man called Wheeler, stoically put up with our frenzied moving about of furniture and general breaking up of his clockwork routine. We rehearsed over and over, selecting various representative guests and staff and making them run through their brief lines till everything was perfect. I myself had a plane standing by in the snow to carry me back to Montreal for another broadcasting engagement immediately this was over.

Our main idea was to capture the atmosphere of young Canada on holiday in the snow. Children had to be interviewed and an instructor had to be found to ring a handbell, calling them to skiing lessons. Then the cables began to flash ever faster across the Atlantic. The planners at Broadcasting House had decided to cut our time from four to three minutes. The next day it was reduced from three to two minutes. And on Christmas Eve we received the final blow.

The B.B.C. could only give us a minute on the air. Guests who had patiently rehearsed their lines, staff who had borne our intrusions with fortitude, had to be told that they would not be needed for the broadcast, after all. To my horror I found that one or two of the guests whom I had agreed to interview had gone to the trouble to notify their friends and relations across the width and breadth of Canada. One girl had even telephoned her mother and father in Chislehurst, England, telling them to stand by to hear her on Christmas Day. I turned somersaults in my attempts to keep her in and did actually get her a few seconds on the air. It was extraordinary to stand with headphones in that Canadian mountain hotel and listen to the engineers and producers in London and the various other points in the Empire discussing the mechanics of the big Commonwealth hook-up. Somehow, it went off all right and there were no hard feelings and no bones broken when the amiable Mr. Wheeler nearly drowned us all in a sea of Scotch and rye whisky. I hurried off to the waiting aircraft with extreme reluctance.

I went into the United States as often as I possibly could, confining my travels largely to the northern parts. I would very much have liked to spend some time south of the Mason-Dixon line, but on the whole I am glad I did not, because even in the north the prejudice against coloured people is painful and to me inexplicable.

John Salt, who was head of the B.B.C.'s New York office, came to me seething with anger one afternoon. He told me how he had just taken a distinguished American scholar who happened to be coloured, to lunch at a flash restaurant in the Rockefeller Centre. For over an hour he and his guest were unable to obtain a seat. When he persisted, he was eventually given a corner table and ignored. When Salt then told the proprietor that he would sit there till they were served, an angry Italian waiter brought soup and putting a plate down in front of the black man, spat in it.

In Detroit, where the coloured people suffer less than in

most places from racial discrimination, the young negroes tend to reverse the procedure. Ganging up in threes and fours they saunter along, taking up all the pavement room, and push whites into the gutter. One evening I saw a group of coloured lads moving slowly towards me and held my ground.

"Out of our path, Mister," one six-footer said to me.

"Not on your life, my boy," I retorted. "I have never done any harm to a coloured man and so I don't propose to take any nonsense from you."

"Say, lissen, are you a Limey?" I was asked.

"I certainly am an Englishman," I said.

"You guys have got a bad record for the way you treat coloured folks in the British Empire," said six-foot sullenly.

"I don't know about that," I said angrily. "All I have to say is that I haven't done you any harm and have no intention of doing you any, so make way, will you?"

"He's all right," one of the other boys said.

"Sure he's all right," the big fellow said handsomely. "Shake, bud. No offence meant." So we shook hands all round and I was allowed to go on my way.

With Gerald Noxon, a Canadian I first met at Cambridge, I crossed the Niagara river to have a spree in Buffalo on July 4. In a pleasant bar in that really lovely town my "English accent" soon attracted some attention among the patrons who were busily and vociferously celebrating Independence Day. Soon I was listening to one or two violently offensive attacks on General Montgomery, obviously in the hope of drawing my fire. I did not particularly mind what was being said, but I did object to the intention with which they were made. Feelings began to run high. As is always the case if one takes the trouble to find out, there are many more pleasant people in the world than unpleasant ones and after a few brisk exchanges I found myself persuading the assembled company to sing "God Save the King." Americans know the tune because they sing it to the words, "My country 'tis of thee," but I really began to feel I was making headway when I managed to get

everyone to sing "Land of Hope and Glory" on the under-
standing that we could mean what land we liked. The evening
finished on my being woken up on a grass verge by a kindly
policeman who told me I couldn't spend the night in the U.S.—
at least, not on that spot.

I was quite ready to come home when, in 1947, the B.B.C.
decided that my turn in Canada—already considerably
extended—had better come to an end. At a farewell party
in Montreal I was introduced to the chairman of a famous
Canadian watchmaking firm. Seeing me pull out my grandfather's turnip, which I had taken in exchange for my own
from Mother on the night of my departure for Canada, he
let out a cry of pained horror.

"You can't possibly go around with that ancient time-
piece," he told me. "Why don't you get one of our famous
up-to-the-minute wrist watches?"

"I wouldn't be seen dead with one," I said.

"You wouldn't? Well, just for that I'll make you a present
of one."

"If you do I'll sling it in the Atlantic the moment I get
aboard my ship."

"Now, you wouldn't want to do that, friend," the man
remonstrated. "They're perfectly good watches."

"Go away," I told him.

"But, friend, you must accept one of our watches as a
gift. Have you always gone around with that old turnip?"

"If you must know," I replied, "I swapped my wrist watch
with my mother and it is still with her in London, England."

"Well," beamed the man, "in that case you must let me
present your mother with one of our finest watches."

"Go away," I again told the pest. "I like neither you nor
your watches."

After one last delirious fling in New York I found myself
at sea, heading for England and home. Noticing a small
parcel which must have been delivered before we sailed I
picked it up and opened it. Inside were two splendid wrist

156

"A strident problem child."

Ghislaine Alexander, Jerry Desmonde, Elizabeth Allan, G.H.

Photograph: John

"But I do wish that the future were over."

watches with a note from the persistent watchmaker: "Best wishes to you and your mother and I hope you will find the enclosed satisfactory."

I must admit that, to date, neither Mother nor I have had any reason to complain about the man's time-pieces.

17

THE problem now was: what to do next? I was on the unestablished staff of the B.B.C., and the Corporation was getting rid of people rather than taking them on. There was no room for me in my old department of Outside Broadcasting, so for a while I was attached to the Overseas Service. Soon there was to come a great stroke of good fortune, but the first few weeks following my return from Canada were dreary and full of frustration.

By now I knew I had enough broadcasting experience to play a leading part in popular radio features, providing those features needed an expert talker. By this I do not mean a prettifier of polite language: the B.B.C. is surfeited with such mannered gentry. I mean one who is willing to speak up and speak out without undue circumlocution or ambiguity; someone, in fact, willing to call a spade a spade.

My old colleagues, Stewart MacPherson, Richard Dimbleby, Wynford Vaughan Thomas, Raymond Glendenning, and the rest, were now star performers. While I had been working in Canada in comparative obscurity, these fine radio craftsmen had become established in the public mind and heart as household names. And I? Well, for a time it seemed I would either find myself jobless or shelved in some obscure department relaying potted culture to tribesmen.

From time to time I would be interviewed for permanent jobs on the staff. Being unsuccessful in those I wanted and quite unable to accept the ones they offered me, I felt myself becoming more and more of a square peg. It did not appeal to me to become a writer of news bulletins in Basic English for translation into Japanese. Nor was I attracted by the idea of becoming an assistant producer of broadcasts to Bulgaria in the European Service.

The prospect of freelancing had now to be considered and this I faced with the gravest misgiving. I was horrified by the sight of out-of-work actors and B.B.C. rejects who spent their lives in pubs near Broadcasting House, hoping to catch the eye of a producer who might give them work. It would be equally humiliating to make the rounds of offices only to hear that the man you had gone to see regretted but there was nothing for you at present but if you would draft out a few ideas he might be able to do something one day. It is not in my nature, I fear, to accept these bland "brush-offs" with patient good humour. Neither am I able to dispense the smarmy compliments which so many of these people expect for being in a position to say "yes" or "no" to your offers of ideas, time and talent.

Still, I was in a fairly strong position. I had, after all, a few colleagues at Broadcasting House who knew my working background and the kind of media to which I made the most effective contribution. Then, one day, I heard some news which made the prospect of freelancing inevitable. The very popular Transatlantic Quiz, which had been carried on between a London team and a team in New York, had to be abandoned by the B.B.C., owing to lack of dollars. The Corporation wanted something to put in its place. So Bill Newton, who had been B.B.C. representative in Chicago, conceived what turned out to be the bright idea of a Round Britain Quiz on the same lines as the Transatlantic Quiz. Only this time, while the home team was still based in London, I was to go around the regions as a kind of peripatetic question master, a poor man's Alistair Cooke.

On the evening of November 1, 1947, I caught the night train from London to Glasgow—the first of countless overnight journeys in the course of this exhausting, exasperating, but on the whole most enjoyable programme, which, to date, is still going strong.

After shaving at the station hotel and breakfasting on wholesome Scots food, I stepped into the sparkling Glasgow morning and walked across to the office of Gordon Gildard, Head of Scottish Programmes. There we discussed last-minute details of the quiz, then still very much an unknown quantity. We then went off to lunch with the Scottish team, James (now Sir James) Fergusson and Jack House, both of whom I found delightful company. House is a Glasgow journalist with a lively mind and ready wit, who endeared himself to me. When I asked how listeners would be able to distinguish between their (to me) somewhat similar Scots accents, he replied:

"I don't think they'll find any difficulty. James speaks with a public school accent, while mine is a public house one."

Fergusson is eighth baronet of Kilkerran, a grave serious-minded Old Etonian, and Keeper of the Records of Scotland. Literary questions are his particular favourites and he has an astounding memory for the phrases and characters of the classical English writers.

There were to be two recordings that afternoon. While the London team of Denis Brogan and Hubert Phillips assembled with their Question Master, Lionel Hale, in a studio at Broadcasting House, we went off to a studio in the Glasgow office and waited for the engineers to link us with London. When this was done we went into a trial run, using questions which the producer and we two Question Masters had rejected as unsuitable for actual broadcasting. This served to warm up the teams before the recording proper and also give the technical staff the chance to balance up the sound and make other tests.

At one point I was slightly disconcerted. After asking a somewhat lengthy question I heard an engineer's voice say:

"I'm afraid Mr. Harding is making more noise than the two teams put together."

Before giving him a piece of my mind I glanced down at the microphone. It was much too close. Pushing the mike back about a foot, I repeated the question. There were no further comments from the worthy technical experts.

160

The questions chosen for the warm-up were fairly easy ones, picked deliberately to give the teams confidence. Unfortunately, the second one from Lionel Hale completely baffled my team. It was, I think, connected with a simple point of historical fact and was asked with full formality. I hastily suggested we scrubbed that one out and went on to my next elementary teaser. We have since found that this is one of the most baffling aspects of this snag-ridden programme. We usually like to open and close with comparatively easy questions, the idea being that this ensures a brisk start and avoids trailing off at the end. All too frequently these questions, beamed at a team member with specialized knowledge of the subject, fail to register. On the other hand, the next question, deliberately picked to give the recipients an uncomfortable time, is likely to be answered almost before one has finished asking it. A Quiz Master must be exceptionally stern about this, checking a too swift reply in order to give listeners time to at least absorb the question before having the answer blurted out for them.

Two minutes before three o'clock we wound up the trial run. I settled back in my chair and waited. Each one of us was wearing headphones but presumably the same tension was making itself felt in the London studio, for we sat there in sudden complete silence. Then we heard the voice of the producer, in London, say: "All right, everybody. Ten seconds to go."

We continued to sit in silence. I gazed at the team, the team gazing back at me. Dead silence. The green light in the studio went on, indicating that the recording had started. For the first time I heard Lionel Hale's cheery voice saying:

"Are you there, Glasgow? Hello, Gilbert Harding. Here are Denis Brogan and Hubert Phillips in the London studio. How are you up there across the Border?"

"We're very well, thank you," I replied. "James Fergusson and Jack House are both here and waiting to hear the first question from you." *Round Britain Quiz* was on the air.

The programme caught on very well, and three successive Controllers of the Light Programme have been pleased with it ever since. The routine soon evolved into a familiar pattern. London would be challenged for a series of eight weekly contests (recorded in four batches of two) by each of the regions in turn, with Dublin as an occasional "extra." The rota, which was kept flexible, has been: Scotland, Wales, West, North, Northern Ireland and Midland, the aim being to avoid consecutive programmes from adjoining regions.

A curious remote-control kind of good-fellowship sprang up between the teams, and when Lionel Hale became seriously ill we all missed him enormously. He kept in touch with us, however, all through the many months he spent in hospital and helped us considerably. We get about three hundred suggestions each week from listeners. About one in ten is potentially useful, and this cream was sent to Hale, who edited them from his sick bed, polishing and arranging the lists. He would send enough for two programmes at a time, these arriving usually a week before the recording date. I would then go through the questions and answers with the producer, usually in the company of the other Quiz Master. (Peter Watson and then Leonard Sachs deputized for Hale.) The producer would screen out any questions to which I, or my London opposite number, objected for personal reasons or because they might cause "policy" trouble. The B.B.C. take great pains to avoid giving offence to listeners on grounds of religion, health, public morals and taste in general, and I—and my colleagues—are constantly on the watch for possible breaches of these unwritten rules in such programmes as *Round Britain Quiz*.

At first I thoroughly enjoyed travelling by plane and train across the country. After a while, this nomad existence of living in hotels and out of a trusty and much battered suitcase, became not so much irksome as terribly wearing. I would—and still do—find myself going to sleep in the middle of conversations. Then, on getting between the sheets, sheer fatigue keeps me awake. The strain of taking part in an endless succession of broadcasts places an extra tax on one's health and strength. (After all, even recorded programmes must be flawless, since mistakes involving further recordings and overtime are extremely costly.) Fortunately, I have always managed to find some solace from my friends in the various regions and from the sudden moments of elation when one knows the programme has been extra good. Among the many gifted and charming people who have taken part in these quizzes I have particularly happy memories of the following.

Though I have never been "on their side," I never fail to be impressed by the remarkable team work of Denis Brogan and Hubert Phillips in London. Each has his pet subjects, and each willingly admits that one without the other would feel quite lost. Hubert Phillips is best at dealing with questions on astronomy, botany, bridge, mathematics, chemistry and physics, and the works of Lewis Carroll. Brogan, on the other hand, is rarely stumped by any questions dealing with French or American history (however obscure) and can recite not only the list of American Presidents since Washington (which is not beyond the grasp of the average schoolboy) but of the Vice-Presidents as well—though he has been a bit shaky about the 1870's.

The Welsh team is brilliantly represented by Wyn Griffith, who is a Treasury official, civil servant and a man of letters, and T. I. Ellis, a tall academic man, son of a great Welsh leader, who teaches at the University of Wales.

Another university man, James Boyce, with Ronald Green, a Government civil servant in Northern Ireland, is a formidable challenger of the London team. I have long given up worrying about difficult questions, a practice which I abandoned after Boyce answered what I consider the stiffest three-part question ever asked in *Round Britain Quiz*. I strongly objected to its inclusion and only accepted with misgiving when it was pointed out that the answers each had the same initial letter, a clue which might possibly help if the quizee noticed it. I also knew that Boyce, one of the two people who would have

163

to try to find the answers, had recently produced a play written by one of the people involved in the questions. Having "planted" these clues with the reader, I still doubt whether they will find the correct answers to the questions, which were as follows:

1. Who asked for the return of 18,000 men?
2. Who commemorated a famous victory and was also responsible for a Confederacy?
3. Whose first royal request was for thirty minutes alone?

When the time came for Lionel Hale to ask these questions I fully expected that they would leave the Northern Ireland team speechless. Dutifully I repeated them and almost before the words had left my lips James Boyce could be heard muttering:

"Confederacy? Confederacy? That must be Vanbrugh. Yes, Sir John Vanbrugh, architect and dramatist. Of course, I acted in his play *The Confederacy*. Oh, and as an architect he was responsible for building Blenheim Palace for the first Duke of Marlborough, to commemorate the famous victory at Blenheim."

"Right, James Boyce," Lionel Hale said from London. "One mark. Now would you like to try again?"

Boyce did not hesitate.

"Surely," he said. "Now, let me see—was it not Queen Victoria who said after her succession, to her mother: 'And now, pray, leave me alone for thirty minutes,' or words to that effect?"

"It was indeed, James Boyce," said Hale delightedly. "Do you think you could go on to the next question?"

"Now you've stumped me there, I think," said Boyce. "You want to know who asked for the return of eighteen thousand men?"

At this point I said: "I think it is in order for me to point out that the names of all three subjects have the same initial letter. Correct, Lionel Hale?"

"That is quite correct, Gilbert Harding," replied Hale.

"Let's think now," said Boyce. "Victoria, Vanbrugh—now, who else is there? Voltaire. Marguerite de Valois. Verdi. Vilepoi, now he was a soldier but I don't remember anything about him asking for the return of eighteen thousand men. Eighteen thousand men? There must be a massive clue in that, somewhere."

"It might help," I said quietly, "if you divide this figure by three."

"Six thousand men?" Boyce asked. "Six thousand—why, that's the number for a Roman legion, isn't it. Just a moment now V? V? Valerian? No. Ah, yes—Varus. Publius Quintilius Varus, the Roman general who was ambushed by Arminius the German chief, and was routed with three legions. He called upon them to return but they went on running, whereupon he killed himself."

"Right again," said Lionel Hale. "Three marks, James Boyce."

"He deserves a dozen," I growled.

"He certainly does," Hale agreed. "But three's the limit. Now for the next question . . ."

One may as well admit that each Question Master does what he can, within limits, to help his team along. But in this instance I think Hale was as excited as I was by this fine display of erudition. At the time, Boyce did not think he had done anything spectacular. On another occasion, after two fairly routine recordings of the programme he was so exhausted at the end that we had to lead him to an anteroom and stretch him out on a couch for half an hour's complete rest. Such are the strains of broadcasting.

I regret to say that we no longer go to Dublin where there was the admirable team of Noel Peart, a practising barrister at the Irish Bar, and Alec Newman, a leader writer on the *Irish Times*. Peart, a Roman Catholic, and Newman, a Protestant, made an admirable combination. They enjoyed the programme as much as I enjoyed having them as a team, and they were extremely popular with listeners everywhere.

That the programme fell a victim to narrow, paltry nationalism was a great pity.

The Northern Irish objected to the inclusion of a team from Dublin in a programme called *Round Britain Quiz* on the grounds that the Republic made much of the fact that it was no longer part of Great Britain. The Republican Government in Dublin likewise complained that we could not possibly include them, and for the same reason. (North and South were at least in agreement on this point!) I found a formula which satisfied them for a bit. When we recorded from Dublin I would open the programme by saying: "This week we are leaving the United Kingdom and going to Ireland." But in the end nothing could appease the particular vanities north and south of the border and we had to give it up, but only after a dreary competition in stupidity out of which no one came off very well.

18

WHEN, to the surprise of several knowledgeable people at Broadcasting House, *Round Britain Quiz* became established as a popular radio programme and (to the further surprise of these Cassandras) Gilbert Harding settled without undue difficulty into the job of travelling Quiz Master, it became imperative that I leave the B.B.C. staff.

I wondered, at the time, why the B.B.C. should want to pay me much more for being off the staff than on, and for keeping to a less strict time-table. Now, of course, I realize that they are quite right in their policy of having as few "name" broadcasters on the staff as possible. After all, if you have a house and garden big enough you might employ a full-time gardener, but you would not employ a full-time doctor. In the same way, the B.B.C. sensibly insists that specialists (e.g., Quiz Masters) of any kind should be available for fees rather than on the permanent pay roll—where they are all too apt to be entangled by interdepartmental tussles for their services.

I could not help being worried (as I still am) by the loss of permanent regular employment and with it the possibility of a pension. So far it has been all right, but there is always the horrible feeling that one of these days someone will have had enough, and that will be that. Nothing is shorter than the public memory and nothing more fleeting than the phoney inflated reputations of radio.

The problems of free-lancing, not always immediately apparent, soon became so. In the first place, on leaving the staff, I missed the services of a secretary. Then, as I found myself struggling to cope with engagements, correspondence and travel arrangements from the limited confinement of a

167

small flat in one of London's outer suburbs, I began to realize just how indispensable those unobtrusively offered, casually accepted B.B.C. services really are.

Each time I lifted the telephone in my flat to ring Belfast or Glasgow—or merely a B.B.C. colleague in London—I began to feel like the prudent man who takes a taxi and then cannot keep his eye off the meter. Each time I sat down to write a letter (and there were hundreds to deal with) I missed the supplies of envelopes, notepaper, pens, ink, typewriter ribbons, erasers, rulers and the rest which an indulgent Corporation would conjure up for me even before I had run out of existing stock. To the common exasperation of present-day travel, eating and living, was added this large spectre of having to do one's own office work and finance it all from one's own pocket. This meant only one thing: I would have to work harder than ever before, accept all offers, tackle any reasonably well-paid job, in order to keep the one-man firm of Harding Inc. solvent and the tax collectors happy.

Still, I had made a good start with a weekly quiz programme and now I was beginning to hear of other likely broadcasting jobs. The best of these came my way shortly after *Round Britain Quiz* was launched. The B.B.C. wanted a Question Master for a revived series of the *Brains Trust* and I was given the job.

I enjoyed every moment of this job, even though the first time I reported as Question Master I arrived at the studio with two black eyes and a split lip. A day or two before the broadcast, thinking that I could run faster than a bus, I seized the rail as it was moving from a stop. At that moment the driver chose to accelerate and, losing balance, I fell, my face hitting the footboard. I was dragged along for a hundred yards till the conductor stopped the bus.

Cyril Joad, Bertrand Russell, Lord Samuel and other distinguished brains-trusters were most sympathetic when we met for dinner before the broadcast. I found their company most stimulating and within a few minutes we were all in happy disagreement and so mundane a matter as a damaged face was forgotten as we played conversational ping-pong with the eternal verities.

As Joad often used to say, if only we could have broadcast the talk over the dinner table it might well have provided more entertainment and enlightenment than the actual broadcast. The dinner—and a very good dinner it was, too —would always be given in the Director-General's dining-room on the second floor of Broadcasting House. Afterwards, we would be given a stirrup cup in a duty room. If other engagements did not call us away, the talk would continue here afterwards and I now look back on those occasions with nostalgic delight.

Joad was undoubtedly the most outstanding personality of them all. It is true that everyone did not like him and that his curious high-pitched laugh and somewhat superior mannerisms irritated many, but he had the gift of clarity of analysis and expression and the tremendous virtue of being provocative. You might not always have agreed with him, but you could not ignore what he had to say.

I think it is true to say that when Joad was withdrawn from the *Brains Trust* it began to die. He could always be relied upon to say something which would spark off the others —and some of the others needed it. I missed him greatly. He was one of the few people I have ever known or heard of who really was irreplaceable. Joad was a great loss.

During the dinner we never actually discussed the programme which we were about to do. The broadcast itself was less fun, naturally. No matter how much you become accustomed to broadcasting you never quite lose that sense of tension just before the green light goes on and you know you are "on the air." For me there was the added responsibility of seeing that everyone who wanted to say something had a chance to do so. While one part of my mind was watching the clock, another would be registering what people were saying, how they were saying it, and whether there was any repetition of what had been said. Yet another part of my mind would be attempting to balance the programme, making sure that any member of the panel who so far had said very little would be encouraged to say more fairly soon. Then I would be half forming the sentences which I myself would have to add by way of rounding off the panel's coverage of a subject. There was always the anxiety of having to sum up at the end, neatly and succinctly and possibly with a so-called observation of one's own. In the early days I would look through the questions and try to think of something salty to say only to find that far too often my carefully rehearsed "impromptu" was used by one of the members of the team. That soon convinced me that rehearsed or organized wit is never worth while.

One of the joys of being a bachelor is that one always finds time to do the things one really wants to do. Busy as I was, therefore, I gladly accepted the offer of yet another job which needed a ready talker. This was the programme, *We Beg to Differ*, and I incline to agree with those who say that my public notoriety as a cantankerous, opinionated bachelor originates from those broadcast battles between the sexes. Personally, I am no more critical of women than I am of British Railways, say, or noisy children or hotel cooking.

It was Charmian Innes who first suggested to B.B.C. producer Pat Dixon that a discussion feature in which men and women aired their grievances would make for lively listening. It certainly did. The programme had been running for some time when I was asked to succeed Dr. Charles Hill, "the Radio Doctor," who had to stop broadcasting on becoming a Parliamentary candidate.

The panel of *We Beg to Differ* generally met at Broadcasting House about noon to warm up over a glass of sherry before starting the programme. As with the *Brains Trust*, we never discussed any of the coming questions, though we were free to do so had we wished. There was, however, a sort of *tabu* against it. Most of the participants were in some way or other connected with show business, and, as everyone knows, entertainers are nearly always superstitious—even the ones who claim they are not.

When it was time to face the studio audience the panel would go on to the platform and settle down, the women on the right, the men on the left of the chairman, Roy Plomley. Then there would be the usual ten seconds of tension before the green light, and then the red would precipitate us upon the treacherous waves of sound. (I was becoming used to this by now, but I still felt that momentary stab of queasiness that sometimes happens to the most experienced air traveller just before the aircraft leaves the runway.)

As with *Round Britain Quiz*, I found it fun largely because I enjoyed the fellowship of the panel. I had always adored Gladys Young and now I was finding it difficult to disagree with her sane, straightforward views. It was easier to wrangle with those delightfully witty women, Joyce Grenfell and Charmian Innes. Mrs. Grenfell (her husband, Reginald Grenfell, is a soldierly-looking business executive) is one of those perfectly groomed, disarmingly outspoken products of the Girls' Public School movement, with a flair for putting people at their ease and then encouraging them to "tire the sun with talking." My ideal woman, in fact. Her ability to talk back simply increases my admiration. Charmian Innes, then the bachelor girl of the team, used to turn up wearing the most fantastic hats which were somehow dwarfed by her spectacular and picturesque conversational technique. Sometimes it seemed as if she was deliberately trying to shock everyone with her forthrightness, and I relished her high spirits and uninhibited gaiety.

But before I give the impression of being completely under the spell of my charming opponents, I must explain that the entire spirit of *We Beg to Differ* depended on the genuine respect and affection the opposing teams felt for each other. It was, in the best sense, a marriage of minds. The fact that two of the leading opponents—Kay Hammond and John Clements —are happily married underscores my contention that the

171

programme was highly civilized and friendly. It was always fun to watch the sudden flash of affection in Kay's eyes after she had scored from John—who would counter with some stingingly effective retort. Then the pair would exchange quick private smiles, rather like fencers saying *touché* after a particularly brilliant piece of swordplay which had temporarily equated the contest.

Still, the legend grew that I was a grouch and a woman hater. Feeling so completely at home amongst these charming ladies, what else could I do but give them the full benefit of my accumulated opinion? It would have been churlish to do otherwise. Yet I was asked by the editors of newspapers and glossy periodicals to air my views on women, marriage, divorce, and the education of children. Fortunately, I have always had fairly strong views on all these subjects, so I was able to oblige. It is nonsense to suppose that a confirmed bachelor cannot know anything about home life. Nothing gives me greater pleasure than to spend an evening with a happily married couple whose home is a real one. But whenever I express my views—and, being a bachelor, I have probably had far more time in which to ponder these matters than most married men—someone is always at hand to cry, "Humbug!"

About this time my life literally ceased to be my own. Unlike such colleagues as Elizabeth Allan and Richard Dimbleby, I have no real home or family to retire to when the pressure of work becomes intolerable. I spend most of my time eating in hotels and public restaurants, in travelling by rail, aircraft and motor car across these islands, and in meeting a succession of people most of whom I never expect to see again. I can, therefore, only record what has happened to me as a wandering public notoriety.

The next step towards my becoming what is sometimes nauseatingly called a "radio celebrity" was taken in the early summer of 1950. When Stewart MacPherson left *Twenty Questions* to work in North America, I hoped that I might succeed him in the Question Master's chair. But I was disappointed. Kenneth Horne did it instead and he did it very well.

My chance came when Kenneth took a fortnight's holiday from the programme and I was employed on those two occasions as his stand-in. He very kindly sent me a telegram wishing me success and his good wishes were justified to the extent that when the programme started after a short break, and Kenneth was no longer available, I replaced him.

Twenty Questions is entirely unscripted and (except on rare occasions) unrecorded, yet each week I receive letters from people who swear that the programme is as carefully rehearsed as one of Sir John Gielgud's major Shakespearean productions. They go on to inform me that, since I am obviously in touch with Norman Hackforth, who tells listeners the questions, the team must also be able to hear what Norman is saying. Finally, these queer correspondents challenge me to write back and deny it. Since I never bother to reply to such tomfool letters I dare say that my silence has convinced them that they are right.

What actually happens is this. The team and I usually arrive about twenty minutes before we are due to go on the air. Unless (which is unusual) we are broadcasting from a public place, the transmission is from the Paris Cinema in Lower Regent Street, some two hundred yards from Piccadilly Circus. Earlier in the day I have run through the questions and approved them, but apart from producer Mike Meehan, Maggie Stratton, who sits beside me and helps to check them off and generally give me invaluable assistance, and myself, the only other person who has seen the questions (thought up by Mike) is the B.B.C. typist. The approach to the Studio is invariably bustling with the comings and goings of B.B.C. attendants, visitors, and friends of the team who have to be found seats. As in the case of my other programmes, those of us taking part make a point of never discussing the coming broadcast. By the time Anona Wynn, Joy Adamson,

Richard Dimbleby, Jack Train and Norman Hackforth have said "hello" it is time to line up to take our bow on the studio platform.

Norman, having been given his list containing questions only (he does not need to know the answers) hurries off to his soundproof cubicle in another part of the building and Mike steps up on the platform and proceeds to "warm up" the studio audience by explaining the "drill" about applause, laughter, and so on.

Dimbleby follows with a little speech to emphasize Mike's points and tell the audience something about the rest of us. He then beckons to Anona, who is waiting at the studio entrance, and brings her on to the platform to be introduced. Anona acknowledges the inevitable applause and crosses to her seat behind the team's bench, a long narrow table on which are placed four microphones and four glasses of water and one *carafe* filled to the brim with this delectable liquid.

My bench, which faces the team's, contains one microphone, one set of headphones, and a *carafe* and two glasses for Maggie and myself, should I feel the compulsion to pour myself a nip of the London Water Board's unadulterated H_2O. Our benches, by the way, are situated a good ten paces away from one another with the team's on the audience's left and mine on its right.

Joy Adamson and Jack Train follow Anona, then Dimbleby introduces Maggie, who comes in carrying the file of questions and two stop-watches. Finally I am introduced and Dimbleby dashes off to his seat beside the team and I go to my seat beside Maggie. Mike Meehan is by now seated at his producer's panel at the far end of the stage and with about fifty seconds to go, I place the headphones over my ears and wait for zero hour—not without the usual, and by now almost friendly, sensation of being about to take off in an aircraft.

Twenty seconds to go. Fifteen. Maggie has everything laid out beside me. Twelve seconds. The card containing the first question is firmly in my hand. Ten seconds. The green light flashes. Five seconds. Three. Two. The red light begins to glow and I begin to talk. Another *Twenty Questions* is on the air.

I never cease to wonder at the splendidly orchestrated combination of brains, wit and erudition that each week faces me across the microphones in the studio. Dimbleby, seismic with humour, profound, analytical and always courteous. Anona, whose uncanny telepathic powers sometimes leave a swift psychic chill on the air, as if a fifth shadow-mind had briefly joined the panel. The cheerful, cheeky gaiety of Jack Train, who knows all about sport and frequently arrives skimming the evening newspapers for last-minute topicality. Joy Adamson, Scottish, thorough, intensely feminine, whose inspired probings unerringly locate the buried answers.

If, as is the way of all radio things, *Twenty Questions* is ever shelved away, I shall chiefly miss this intangible *camaraderie* of the mind which so enlivens my Monday evenings. Though these four people work individually, they have the spirit of a good team, and are never out to "get" their colleagues in order to earn individual kudos.

There have, of course, been hitches. On one or two occasions the attendants who carry in the boards telling the studio audience what the objects are, have held them sideways and given the team an inadvertent chance to see what was written on them. When this has happened, the team—or whoever may have seen the board—says: "Sorry, we couldn't help seeing the object." And we go on to the next one. This has only happened twice, to my knowledge. On another occasion Jack overheard members of the studio audience mention the object aloud. He immediately told me and we instantly went on to the next object.

We all have our idiosyncrasies and pet hates. I personally dislike questions dealing with astronomy. The team has sometimes boggled at certain objects which we have brought up many times . . . invisible ink . . . laundry marks . . . agony columns . . . the rope in the Indian rope trick. Despite my telling them, after the first time of asking, that they had failed to get the answer previously, the team suddenly reveals a curious "blind spot" about these repeat objects. On one occasion, however, the team were given fifteen objects and got every one, including such completely unrelated items as a brass bedstead, junket, water wings, pigs' trotters, a posy and Admiral van Tromp.

During the Christmas holiday of 1952 the team decided to reverse the procedure and give *me* a solo set of twenty questions. With considerable help from Dimbleby, who had taken over my headphones for the occasion, I got the object with my nineteenth question. It was: Forces' Sweetheart. Never again.

I have already written of the strain involved in making several broadcasts each week, year after year. Now I must turn to one of the less fortunate results of prolonged mental and physical pressure. It is something which I would prefer to forget, but having committed myself so far, I shall try to complete what I hope will be an honest record of my life. I refer, of course, to the night I lost my temper in the *Twenty Questions* programme.

I was perfectly sober that night, but I had had a frustrating, wearing day during which everything seemed to have gone wrong. I arrived at the studio late, a thing which rarely happens and, when it does, is always a source of extreme anxiety and nervous tension. With only thirty seconds to go I hurried across to my Question Master's bench, ignoring the audience to whom I was being introduced.

Then one of those dreadful things that used to happen in the films of W. G. Fields happened to me. I got into a terrible muddle with the headphones. The cord became tangled and, try as I would, I somehow could not get it sorted out. I sighed and groaned and muttered—most men in my position would have been swearing aloud. Then, seeing the studio red light flicker to show that we were on the air, I tugged at the cord in a sort of split-second panic and dropped the headphones, causing such a clatter that listeners must have thought they had tuned in to a prize fight.

As a result, the announcer who, a few seconds earlier, had introduced the programme cut us off, saying: "They do not seem to be quite ready for us in the *Twenty Questions* studio." A minute later, the headphones were untangled and the programme began. Now I suppose that having started on the left foot, as it were, I should have resolved to take whatever came next meekly and calmly, but the day's accumulation of petty irritations ending with the farce of the tangled headphones had aggravated my temper to the point of no return.

One of the objects was, "A Peony." Jack Train guessed it fairly early. He shouted: "A Peony . . . A Peony!" But fate conspired against me. Handicapped by the headphones, I frequently have to request less noise from the studio audience in order to hear what is said in my ears. Jack's enthusiasm must have moved the audience to applause and I, in the general commotion, motioned them to remain silent and went on with the game. The panel exhausted their twenty questions, and when I announced the object, Jack naturally protested that he had already guessed it. By this time I was in no mood for complaints and somewhat brusquely said: "Never mind, let's get on with the next question."

The programme limped on and, at the end, when I should have announced the result, I said with considerable acerbity: "I suppose I ought to let you know the score. If you've been listening you won't need it, and if you haven't you won't want it anyway!"

I make no other comment than to say that I was suspended from *Twenty Questions* for several months.

My work was now taking me over thousands of miles of territory each year, and there were weeks on end when I literally lived out of a suitcase. On the whole, I cannot complain of the kindly treatment and friendly assistance I have been given during my travels. I am particularly grateful to the hotel keepers in Edinburgh, Glasgow, Belfast and Cardiff who always

177

make one very comfortable and have learnt to tolerate one's idiosyncrasies. These gentlemen most considerately pander to my Transatlantic tastes, which make a hotel bedroom without a private bathroom intolerable, a bedside telephone essential, and a good supply of thick towels desirable.

Railways—British Railways—are a different matter. I never know what to think of them. One's feelings towards them are those of a fond parent towards a wayward son, darting helplessly between affection and exasperation. I have given up trying to understand why on some trains one can find really good food and excellent service, and on others be given grudgingly served filth. One thing I do know is that British Railways deserve a very small proportion of the criticism levelled against them. I have found that if one does as they ask and reports bad service, the Hotels Executive tries its best to put it right; but what is more important is to report *good* service, which so often goes unrewarded and unacknowledged. As a nation we should be much better fed if we dropped the dreary middle-class idea that it is vulgar to comment on the food offered in public places. If only people would praise and thank when they feel like it, and blame and criticize when they feel they are being sold short, the standard of public service would go up immediately.

On one occasion my habit of thanking people for services rendered had a somewhat disconcerting effect all round. I was in Belfast for a recording of *Round Britain Quiz* and had taken some friends to a hotel restaurant where I was astonished to be given a really splendid first-class luncheon. So good was it, in fact, that we sent for the chef—a Swiss— and offered him our thanks and praise and a glass of champagne. Months later I returned to the hotel and was puzzled to find the food commonplace and indifferently prepared. Calling the manager, I asked:

"What has happened to the chef?"

"He's gone, sir," the manager said reproachfully.

"Gone? Why?"

"It's all your fault, sir."

"How could it be my fault?" I said. "The last time I was here we got along very well together."

"That's the trouble," said the manager, "you made too much fuss of him. Since then no one has said anything good or bad about his cooking, so last week he gave his notice."

"What on earth for?"

The manager shrugged. "He said people over here don't care about food and are not worth cooking for. The only man who ever praised him"—the manager pointed accusingly at me—"did so on one of his 'off' days. It made him so homesick for the Continent that he decided to go back. Now we've got to put up with what we can get."

"Oh, no," I said, rising. "You may have to, but I won't. You can send this food back to the new chef—without my compliments."

By the early summer of 1951 my life had almost set in its present routine—if one can call this frantic business of being shuttled from one corner to another of this land, of walking the tightrope of incessant broadcasting, of being slapped on the back and poked in the chest by curious strangers, a routine. At least I was beginning to manage my affairs. I was still living at Twickenham. When I came back from Canada in 1947 my mother and sister were occupying the flat. Since it was not big enough for three, Mother went to live with her sister in Hereford and, not without misgiving, Constance and I shared the flat as we had done before the war. A secretary came three or four times a week to deal with my ever-growing correspondence and I just managed to go about my business without setting up a home nearer the middle of London. It was a strain, but I managed. Then I heard a piece of news which (though of small interest to me at the time) was to precipitate me into the ultimate heights and depths of public notoriety.

I had made several fugitive appearances upon the Television screen. On one or two occasions I had joined Daphne Padel, Harold Warrender and Ted Kavanagh in a TV parlour game

179

connected with the solving of crossword puzzles. But I had not made any marked impact in this medium.

Then, one day, Ronald Waldman, Head of B.B.C. Television Variety, told me he was considering a new parlour game which he thought might suit me. On the face of it, it didn't seem very exciting. It seemed awfully dreary to me to have four people trying to guess the job of the panel beaters—and perhaps it is. But the transformation of *What's My Line?* from a sickly infant to a strutting, strident problem child surprised everyone, myself included. Myself, perhaps, more than anyone!

19

ONE overcast evening towards the end of May, 1951, I drove to the B.B.C.'s new Television studios at Lime Grove, Shepherd's Bush. I had been invited to see the telefilm of this new quiz which had just been flown over from the United States. Having already heard an unimpressive sound recording of this show, I arrived at the studios convinced that I was wasting my time.

Several other people had been asked along. I greeted old friends like Ted Kavanagh and Jerry Desmonde, Barbara Kelly was there also, and Frances Day. A rising young Dubliner called Eamonn Andrews sat in one corner of the small viewing theatre and I was also happy to see Major Bill O'Bryen, representing his wife, Elizabeth Allan. Presiding over us all was our host, Ronald Waldman, and also in attendance was T. Leslie Jackson, producer-designate of the British version of the show we were about to see—that is if we managed to evolve a British version. At that stage, everything was extremely tentative and the only person with his fingers crossed was Maurice Winnick, who owned the British rights of this U.S. patented property.

The lights dimmed and the screen lit up with a picture of four grim-looking Americans gazing biliously at a Question Master. After some preliminary chit-chat a muscular representative of the American industrial classes appeared and, unaided by any preliminary mime, the four gloomy members of the panel began making attempts to guess the muscular one's occupation. It seemed extremely dreary to me and I cannot remember much more about the telefilm because I almost fell asleep in my chair.

Up went the lights again and we began to discuss what

some of us had seen. Suddenly I brightened. I thought there might be possibilities, after all. What had bothered me about the film was the manifest puerility of four adults trying to guess a person's job—and invariably a pretty puerile job, at that. Now it seemed to me that everything rested on the Question Master's insight. As long as he did not take these jobs too seriously the whole thing could flare up into a spirited, good-natured parlour affair on the lines of *Twenty Questions*. So when Waldman asked for my opinion, I told him I thought there were possibilities—if I could be Question Master.

As I invariably do, I seemed to have put my foot into things. It soon became clear that I had not been under serious consideration for the role of Question Master, only as a possible for the panel. Waldman is a fair-minded man, however, and since I had thrown this unexpected spanner into the works he promised to consider my claim. After further talk the gathering dispersed and for several days I heard little more about *What's My Line?*

I was finding work strenuous enough without caring too much whether I tackled yet another job, and in a field other than radio. I have no inherent liking for cameras, hot arc lamps, and being made up. None of these things was needed for sound broadcasting, and I was perfectly content with the progress I had made as a broadcaster since that day at Evesham when I first heard the sound of my own voice and loathed what I heard. There is, after all, a certain pleasure in mastering a job and doing it reasonably well. I had mastered the microphone. Was it really necessary to go on to TV?

One afternoon at my club, a country member, whose name I do not recall, approached me with what has become with me the most tedious of all opening gambits.

"I heard you on the radio last night, old man."

I grunted something suitably ambiguous.

"You are a card, old man. Really you are. You know, as I sat listening, I thought what a pity it was you don't appear on television. Hearing your voice was not enough. Knowing what you look like, I could picture how much more effective you'd have been in vision."

"Ghastly thought," I said.

The conversation stuck in my mind. I have no illusions about my appearance. As a challenger on *What's My Line?* has quite rightly observed, I am no oil painting. It would be a dull world, though, if everyone who lacked film star grace and charm decided to give up the struggle for life. So when Waldman next spoke to me about the programme I was inclined to listen. A compromise had been reached about the matter of a Question Master. Eamonn Andrews was to take the chair for the first programme and I was to follow in the next. I agreed that this was fair.

On Monday, July 16, 1951, the first transmission of *What's My Line?* appeared on the country's television screens. As a prospective Question Master I took no part in the show, but I watched with interest. The panel consisted of Barbara Kelly, Marghanita Laski, Jerry Desmonde and Ted Kavanagh. I found it irritating to see a barrow boy introduced as a street trader, and a woman car driver as a chauffeuse, and I thought everyone was extremely coy about the profession of a cocktail shaker. There was no preliminary mime in those days and the whole thing seemed rather futile, but I still thought there was a chance of brightening the show. The guest celebrities, I remember were the cricketing twins Alec and Eric Bedser. Nothing spectacular about them!

Leslie Jackson and I went carefully through the production arrangements before I took the chair on the following Monday. I arrived early—perhaps too early as things turned out—and was introduced to the challengers. Already, strict security measures were in force to prevent the various competing sections of *What's My Line?* from meeting. (The previous week Jackson had unceremoniously butted his head into one of the Bedsers' midriff when that surprised sportsman attempted to leave his hideout for a minute.) Lime Grove is a vast warren of offices and studios in which it is comparatively easy to keep people segregated.

We interviewed the challengers in one of the large dressing rooms behind the studio from which the programme is sent out. Their order of appearance is always a secret between producer and Quiz Master. In this instance we had devised the following sequence: Water Taster, Artists' Model, Boxer's Second, Guest Celebrity, Male Nurse, Panel Beater. The last, we thought, would be great fun. In industry a panel beater is a skilled craftsman who presses out faults in metal, but we confidently hoped he would also beat our learned panel.

My interviews went remarkably well. Happy at the prospect of doing the job I like most of all (that is, knowing all the answers before I start asking questions) I enjoyed meeting the challengers and we all got along nicely. Meanwhile, in another part of Lime Grove, the panel was trickling in and being installed in their dressing rooms. I then went to my room where a hot meal was brought in from the canteen. Then I was made up for the camera before joining the challengers for a studio rehearsal. Again, all went smoothly.

Returning to my dressing room I carefully studied the cards listing the challengers' names and occupations. This allowed Jackson time to go through a quick studio rehearsal with the panel. He came back to tell me that the guest celebrity had been successfully smuggled in. This is always by way of the goods entrance. Great care is taken to drive the celebrity close up to the entrance and, surrounded by a screen of porters and attendants, whisk him or her to the private make-up room where they must remain till the programme is on the air.

I went round to have a word with the celebrity, in this instance Kathie Beaumont, "the voice of Alice." Walt Disney had just released his film, *Alice in Wonderland*, in this country and Miss Beaumont's picture had been widely published in the press, making her an excellent topical choice. It was then almost time to start. A quick final briefing from Jackson, and

I followed the panel into the studio. Clutched tightly in my hand were the all-important cards. As I sat under the hot bright lamps, waiting to begin, I swiftly ran through the cards again. The order was simple enough. First we would have a batch of three. Easy. Water taster, artists' model, boxer's second. Then Miss Beaumont. Then the male nurse. Finally, if there was still time, we would have fun with the panel trying to guess the panel beater. It was quite possible that this challenger would not come on at all. The programme usually has two "reserves" —who, if not called, come back the following week. One rarely gets through the complete list. "Still," I thought, "we may manage to end on a jolly note with the panel beater." Then the red light went up and the second edition of *What's My Line?* flashed upon the nation's screens.

The first part of the programme went amazingly well. Miss Beaumont made her appearance without mishap. Now all that was left to do was to bring on the male nurse, followed, with luck, by the gallant panel beater, and a pleasant time would have been had by all. But fate decided otherwise.

Challengers in this programme are always summoned by a call boy. Punctual to the second, the next challenger appeared at the entrance and, greeting him amiably, I invited him to write his name on the blackboard. This is, of course, visible on the TV screen. But it was behind me, on my right, and with card number four on the desk before me I left him to it. Glancing once more at the card, I read: Challenger No. 4. Mr. George Benton. Occupation: Male Nurse. What I did *not* know is that the call boy had mistakenly sent in the fifth challenger—Mr. John Morgan. Occupation: Panel Beater.

"Sit down," I said genially after the new arrival had paraded before the panel. (There was no mime in those days, remember.) The gentleman I presumed to be a male nurse then sat down, and guessing began. The panel was soon (I thought) widely off the mark. I did what I could to steer them towards a more reasonable line of inquiry. Short of telling them, though, it seemed that nothing would bring them anywhere near a solution.

The first serious discrepancy occurred when Jerry Desmonde, I think it was, asked:

"Has your job anything to do with transport?"

"Yes," said Mr. Morgan, thinking no doubt of that aspect of his work which involves straightening the metal used in the construction of motor cars.

"No," I said, trying to be fair. Apart from a possible ambulance ride it was highly unlikely that a male nurse had any strong link with transport.

Everyone looked confused, but the guessing went on. Confusion became chaos when someone asked: "Could your job be done equally well by a woman?"

"Yes," said the panel beater, having in mind the many women who do such fine work in industry.

"Oh, no, they could not!" I roared. Women as male nurses indeed!

Things went from bad to worse. Poor Mr. Morgan must have been terribly rattled by my angry contradictions of what he had said. The panel were probably fervently praying for the attention of a nurse, male or female, to soothe their jangled nerves. Listeners, too, must by this time have begun to think they were being treated to a conducted tour of Bedlam.

With everyone plunging through a sea of red herrings the minutes raced by and I suddenly realized it was almost time to wind up the sorry proceedings.

"You have beaten the panel, Mr. Benton," I said curtly.

To the panel I said: "You weren't anywhere near getting an answer. Mr. Benton is a male nurse."

"Oh, no I am not," said the hapless challenger. "My name is Morgan and I'm a panel beater."

"Oh," I said.

Then, with one of those bursts of anger which I find so hard to check, I added: "This is the last time I ever appear on television."

The programme faded out and I was quite resigned to

186

fade from it permanently myself. It was, however, in a state of flux. Nobody, least of all the B.B.C., ever knew until the last few hours who would be called from week to week. There was talk of scrapping it altogether. Viewers were, on the whole, lukewarm about it. Some thought the pace and timing slow, others that it was juvenile. I was as lukewarm about it as anyone.

What's My Line? was, in those days, transmitted on Monday evenings and I already had *Twenty Questions* to do on sound radio. If I was to appear in the television show I had to make a wild four-mile dash by hired car between the Paris Cinema, near Piccadilly Circus, and Lime Grove. London just then was packed with visitors to the Festival of Britain, and it was no joke to rush through that summer's metropolitan traffic and switch from sound to vision, with only a few minutes to spare either way.

Then Liz Allan appeared. Bill O'Bryen, Miss Allan's husband, is a shrewd and seasoned judge of entertainment value. It will be remembered that Bill attended the special showing of the telefilm. Like everyone else, he had reserved judgment on its prospects as a British television hit. Bill had particularly good reasons for not pushing his wife into a poor TV show, Liz having endured a series of disappointments in the theatre since the end of the war. Both however, had taken the trouble to study TV as an entertainment vehicle, and when the enthusiastic and dedicated producer of *What's My Line?*, T. Leslie Jackson, urged Liz to join the panel for a trial run, both Miss Allan and Bill O'Bryen decided to give the programme a try-out.

So, shortly after my unhappy experience in the chair, Jackson lined up a panel consisting of Dorothy Dickson, Elizabeth Allan, Ted Kavanagh and Jerry Desmonde. The advent of Liz was like a breath of spring air in a stuffy tap-room. Her impact was immediate. Viewers wrote and telephoned by the thousand, demanding to see more of this glamorous woman with the engaging mannerisms, well groomed hair,

187

chunky jewellery, attractive dress tops and general air of sophistication and good breeding.

Into the programme there was infused a new brightness and cheerfulness which lifted the dull business of asking dull people dull questions about dull jobs into an amusing game. Within a month, Elizabeth Allan had become one of the first truly great Television stars of her time. And I was invited to return to the panel.

It was tacitly understood that my previous claim to be Question Master had been waived. In any case, Eamonn Andrews had made a remarkably good job of this unenviable task. He has wit, an alert mind, and an abundance of Irish charm. I had no wish to compete with a man I had come to like extremely well, and so I settled down into the programme alongside my colleagues of the panel.

Liz, Jerry Desmonde and I became more or less permanent fixtures. In Miss Allan I found a delightful colleague, and Jerry would always keep things going smoothly with his urbane manner and quiet authority. Several ladies came and went. Brilliant Marghanita Laski has always been too occupied with her writings to find time for regular appearances. Frances Day attracted a faithful following, and I was delighted to discover a fine mind behind her outward allure. Not only is she delightful, de-licious, de-lovely—she is de-learned as well. I shall never forget the occasion when I drove with her to Cheltenham where we were to take part in a brains trust. She had admirable ideas on the way children should be encouraged to read. In the process she revealed a wide knowledge of literature and her views on poetry showed her to be a sensitive and discriminating person, quite unlike the popular view of her as just a musical comedy star. I was always happy to see Barbara Kelly, the talented and attractive wife of Bernard Braden, on the panel.

Weeks passed uneventfully and *What's My Line?* became an established favourite, but there were occasional ripples on the placid surface. Speaking solely for myself, I found some of the situations arising from the questioning of the challengers quite unbearable. I cannot enjoy being misled by muddled thinking. Perhaps I had spent too many years as a schoolmaster.

I always like to be in a position to *know*. As Question Master of *Twenty Questions* and Quiz Master of *Round Britain Quiz* it is I who ask the questions. For that matter, I can face unflinchingly the prospect of interrogating some-one like Richard Dimbleby or Eamonn Andrews. But when I am faced with an unknown "challenger" (the noun is significant) I find it galling to receive oblique and evasive replies to my perfectly straightforward questions.

On the face of it, it seems great fun to ask a perfect stranger what he does for a living. Everyone likes to talk about himself. Indeed, I have had many rewarding exchanges with the charming people who have paid us the great compliment of taking part in *What's My Line?* But it can also be awfully dreary to be one of four people trying to guess the jobs of candy floss spinners, commissionaires, puzzle setters, chambermaids and—in one fantastic instance—sagger makers' bottom knockers!

Never have I attempted to conceal my dislike of middle-class coyness. I abhor circumlocution, genteelisms, "refeened" talk. Therefore, when I am confronted with any of these more deplorable national characteristics, my schoolmaster's gorge rises, and I find myself crossly, but conscientiously, trying to extract clearer responses. Sometimes I get them. At other times I am drawn into arguments about definitions. I cannot help it. The thing is deeply ingrained in me. Also, it is my habit to pay everyone I meet the compliment of regard-ing them as intelligent adults until they prove themselves to be otherwise.

We had our jolly moments. I remember when Peter Kavanagh, the impersonator, was invited along as guest celebrity. Having blindfolded myself, I sat back with the rest of the panel and listened attentively as Eamonn Andrews greeted the (to us) unknown celebrity. Suddenly I was alarmed to hear my own voice speaking! It was a little inflated, as mine is sometimes when I declaim a sonorous passage of prose or a stirring poem.

Frances Day actually exclaimed: "But that's Gilbert using his poetry voice!"

Peter was so good I did not in the least mind the rather obvious leg-pull. Later I learnt that he had taken great pains to get my voice right, even to the extent of making tape recordings of some of my *Twenty Questions* broadcasts and faithfully noting characteristic inflections and favourite forms or usages.

Elizabeth Allan's favourite method of pulling my leg has always been to introduce exotic words, taking great care to pronounce them correctly. Then, having done so, she will turn to me with a quick flash of amusement and watch my reaction. I have not caught her out yet, since her grammar and diction are as impeccable as her hair-style. Liz tends to "take me in hand," giving me an occasional sisterly rap across the knuckles with her pencil if she thinks I have been rather naughty about something or someone.

The guest celebrity is rarely invited to appear in the programme until the last possible moment. This is to avoid the possibility of his or her identity becoming known to the panel beforehand. Even the best-intentioned celebrity cannot always guarantee long-term secrecy. Usually, their agents or their publicity directors must know what they are doing. And it is the business of such people to trumpet their clients' movements abroad, and shout their slightest deeds from the rooftops.

After the show, celebrity and challengers meet Question Master and panel in what the B.B.C. roguishly calls the Hospitality Room. There is usually small-talk about the evening's highlights and a general thawing out over a carefully limited allocation of Scotch whisky and bottled ale. Here I have met such diverse characters as Sam Goldwyn and Prince Monolulu, the racing tipster. Regretfully I must record that on these occasions not one Goldwynism or red hot cert. was vouchsafed me.

Challengers ranging from a knitting needle knobber and tsetse fly sprayer to a black pudding stringer have gathered in the Hospitality Room and enlarged on the wonders of their occupations. Some of the most charming people among them have insisted on pressing upon us samples of their products. Mr. J. W. Dinnage, a trainer of racing donkeys, has been so kind as to present me with a donkey called Dominic, who races regularly and whose welfare is one of the major concerns of my life. With other members of the panel I have received roses from a rose-grower, a turkey from a turkey-breeder, and eggs from a poultry trusser. We have been criticized for accepting such gifts. But why should we refuse gifts from people who have very kindly brought them to us unasked? I certainly do not intend to add to my reputation for rudeness by refusing them.

This business of rudeness is really a bore. An instance of when I was supposed to have been "awkward" occurred on *What's My Line?* when I clashed with a news-vendor. In the course of our attempts to find his occupation, I asked him if he was engaged "in trade or distribution." He said he was not. Afterwards I expressed surprise when we knew his business. I am glad to say that most of the viewers who wrote agreed with me.

It is true that words have different meanings to different people. The word "props," for instance, means different things in a coal mine and a theatre. But I cannot conceive that trade and distribution mean anything but working in a shop (or at a street corner, for that matter) and organizing the distribution of one's wares—which is exactly what every newsagent and paper seller I have known has always done.

Sometimes in this programme I have made what people chose to regard as slighting references to towns or counties. On the brighter side, I must record my gratitude to one

191

northern coastal town. This was when I made the inexcusable blunder of saying I did not know that Fleetwood was a great fishing port. Fleetwood, I am glad to say, did not let forth a childish squeal of rage. On the contrary, someone there decided to confound my ignorance by sending me a parcel of fish. For days after I received this welcome parcel I pondered over the problem of how to work into the next broadcast the phrase: "I wonder what they make at the Mint."

My experiences on *What's My Line?* have convinced me that people with the least sense of humour are civil servants. Not all of them, of course, but my most innocent cracks about them have always brought dozens of angry letters and humourless telephone calls. It was actually proposed at one of their annual meetings that the B.B.C. should restrain comedians and other entertainers from making any reference to the Civil Service. Happily, the motion was lost, which indicates that the majority of civil servants are sane. But one must be constantly on one's guard against such repressive forces. The first thing a dictatorship does is to put its more outspoken clowns and entertainers into concentration camps.

I sometimes wonder whether my grandfather was not right when he despairingly predicted that the only future for me was to become a comic turn on the halls. I am aware that I have come a long way from my original work as question master in such quasi-erudite programmes as *Round Britain Quiz*. My present Jekyll-and-Hyde activities originate, to some extent, from the fact that the B.B.C. has always regarded quiz programmes as a branch of light entertainment, and quite rightly, too. But if these programmes had been part of the talks department there might have been less ambiguity about the status of Quiz Masters, panel members, and suchlike. As it was, I found myself increasingly part and parcel of the great light entertainment set-up. We worked in the world of Frankie Howerd and Archie Andrews. Was it so unreasonable, therefore, that I should find myself joining in their programmes?

It has been fun! Apart from the time I played a comic

policeman in a Frankie Howerd television show, I have never tried to act, or even "put up a show," in public. I just behave as I am and talk as I think, which for some reason appears to be remarkably novel. Yet people continue to think I am "performing" in such programmes as *What's My Line?* Nothing could be further from the truth. The slightest show of individuality, however, brings in shoals of letters from people congratulating me on "the wonderful act you put on the other night!" And if I happen to have avoided any undue exchange of asperities my correspondents reproach me for having failed to "perform."

April Fools' Day, 1952, found me contemplating going out on a provincial tour of a music hall version of *What's My Line?* I was not only in a bad state of "stage fright," but seriously wondering what had become of me. Was this to be the apogee of my career? But when I reached Nottingham I discovered all sorts of charming people working on the same bill. The miseries of a wet day and nervous tensions of a first night in a music hall evaporated as I found myself among clowns, acrobats and jugglers, all working like slaves to wring laughter and applause from the audience. Not for the first time did I realize how remote from reality is the artificial world of TV and radio. Perhaps the kindness with which my colleagues welcomed me backstage was tempered by the fact that they did not take my invasion into their territory as a serious threat. Nevertheless, I began to realize that my grandfather's fateful prophecy had not been as far-fetched as one had thought.

The question of my status as a public entertainer seemed to be bothering others as well. The radio and television correspondent of one newspaper even took the trouble to ask his readers for advice. "Should Harding stick to his last (i.e. asperity, weighty diction, donnish wit, sparkling oratory) or should he pursue his strange new line as a comic?"

I never bothered to find out what, if anything, his readers thought.

20

A FRIEND once told me that he has always thought of my weekly ordeals in *What's My Line?* in terms of a bull-fight. The national sport of Spain is divided into three parts. The first is a ceremonial, ending with the loosing of the bull which is goaded by the short spears of the picadors. In the second the banderillos further irritate the animal by piercing it with darts. In the third the matador stabs the enraged bull to death. Throughout the performance red and other bright colours are worn, and various devices employed to keep the bull angry.

Somewhat cruelly, I think, my *aficionado* friend likens me to the bull. The picadors, he explains, are the challengers, and the studio audience is composed of banderillos. Eamonn Andrews, according to this fanciful interpretation of our parlour game is the matador, remote and cool, with power of life and death over the bull—unless the bull manages to gore him first. Though I cannot entirely agree with this (it makes me far more helpless than I really am), I *have* detected the elemental odours of the bull ring—and of the bear pit—in what is supposed to be a mild Sunday evening's amusement.

In connection with this it is not without significance, I fear, that I have been introduced at a luncheon as the man to whom people tune in—hoping against hope that he will drop an enormous brick. I do not enjoy this sort of reputation, but nothing will persuade me to alter things by trying to "smarm" my way into other people's good books.

Do I really get cross and exasperated with Eamonn Andrews, in particular, and the challengers in general? Yes, of course I do because I am naturally a short-tempered and ill-mannered man—a fact which I recognize and regret. Sorry as I am to disappoint the rumour mongers, I must record the fact that throughout the various runs of *What's My Line?* Eamonn and I have privately remained good friends.

I was once guest at a luncheon of the Radio Industries Club where I found the principal speaker was Eamonn Andrews —and the subject of his talk was "Gilbert Harding." Eamonn made his speech in perfectly harmless and amusing style. Certainly he did not upset me. Of course, I was called upon to reply. In doing so, I was able to tell an Irish story so the affair ended happily. Anyone who went along to that agreeable function expecting fireworks, must have been sorely disappointed.

On another occasion we both agreed to attend a Brains Trust at St. Albans. What we had not realized at the time was that the thing was to take place at midnight on the day before our present Queen's Coronation! Both Eamonn and I had more than enough work to keep us busy in the heart of London during that exciting and momentous Coronation week. But we had given our word to attend and attend we did. Somehow we managed to circumnavigate London's traffic and reach St. Albans in good time, but it was a nerve-racking journey. Under the circumstances it would not have been surprising if two saints had begun to bicker. I am happy to say that everything was sweetness and light. My old TV sparring partner and I even managed to join forces and regale our audience with a duet—the only unharmonious moment of the whole evening.

To my mind one of the most memorable incidents in connection with *What's My Line?* was when the young singer, Gerry Brereton, was introduced to the panel. He had just come down to London and had not made his present name as an entertainer. Apart from a few devoted enthusiasts in the Midlands he was virtually "unknown." Certainly nobody on the panel had ever seen or heard of him before.

I was completely baffled by his mime, which suggested doing something on a typewriter. It soon became clear that he did not work in an office. As I pondered over what he might be doing, I was struck by a certain strangeness about the expression of his face. What could it be? I studied him carefully. He had walked on in a most sprightly fashion, giving an impression of extreme confidence in whatever he was doing. There was something of the smart young business executive about him. He dressed neatly and quietly and looked the picture of dependability and efficiency. Yet there was this slight air of "difference" about him. What was it?

When next it became my turn to interrogate him, I leaned forward and asked quietly:

"Have you lost your sight?"

I sensed a sudden tension in the studio.

"Yes," Brereton replied. "I have."

He spoke without self-pity and the tension passed.

We asked him if he had been typing something in Braille.

"Yes," he said, "that's quite right."

Eventually it was disclosed that he was a singer newly arrived in London to try his luck as an entertainer. The mime was meant to represent him typing out the libretto of a song on a Braille typewriter, which he frequently does.

His movements before the cameras were remarkably accurate. When I discussed this with Brereton later in the Hospitality Room, Leslie Jackson, who happened to be listening, explained how he had twice rehearsed the blind singer on the set that morning. Jackson then told Gerry that the set would remain in position for the rest of the day, and made him welcome to practise as much as he liked.

"That's all right," Brereton had replied. "I know exactly what to do. I stand here beside the stage-brace till I am called. Then I walk straight ahead for three paces till I reach three steps. My left foot comes down on the first of these steps, then when I have got to the top I go forward a couple of paces to reach the blackboard. I pick up the chalk from the rail, sign my name in large letters, put the chalk down, turn round and make two large steps a little to my right, turn right and do the mime.

196

I then step back one pace and I feel the top of the chair with my left hand and I sit down."

"O.K. Gerry, let's see you do it," Jackson had said.

Brereton went through his paces with the utmost confidence.

As we were leaving Lime Grove that night I had personal proof of this remarkable young man's "mental vision."

"Look out, now, Gerry," Jackson said. "We're coming to some steps. There are eleven, altogether."

"No, thirteen," Brereton replied. "I counted them coming in this morning."

As *What's My Line?* found increasing favour with the public I privately found myself becoming increasingly worn out and exasperated. I was still covering hundreds of miles each month as travelling Quiz Master of *Round Britain Quiz*. In addition to *We Beg To Differ* and *Twenty Questions*, I found myself appearing in all sorts of other programmes. Lectures, bazaars, garden fêtes and charity matinées took up what other time I could spare from dealing with correspondence and personal papers. For weeks on end I would find myself "asleep on my feet," snatching what rest I could while travelling in trains, aircraft and cars.

Three days before I was due to appear in the transmission of *What's My Line?* for Sunday, December 7, 1952, I took to my bed with a high temperature and in a state of complete exhaustion. Sometimes I would struggle to my feet and wander about my flat, trying to get into shape for Sunday night. But the slightest movement would cause a severe attack of asthma, and I would collapse back into my bed for a few more hours of uneasy rest. I worried about the many engagements I had broken as a result of my illness, and I am sure I was an extremely bad patient for my long-suffering housekeeper to deal with.

At 11.30 on the Sunday morning I picked up the telephone on my bedside table and told the B.B.C. I was too ill to take part in *What's My Line?* I was asked to turn up if I could, since arrangements had already been greatly upset by a severe London fog, one of the worst for many years. All hands were wanted to man the TV ship, so I promised to make every effort to be there.

Lunch was brought to me in bed and, after a brief nap, I tried to get up. The moment my feet touched the floor I was almost choked by a severe bout of asthma, which was only relieved after I had breathed long and deep into a rubber inhaler. Gingerly I began to dress.

Late that afternoon I shuffled into my sitting room, where a cheery fire was burning. My housekeeper brought me whisky and soda and I poured myself a small 'drink—my first for several days. After two or three sips I began to feel slightly more vigorous and I telephoned a nearby car-hire firm to ask for transport to be sent round in time to get me to Lime Grove for the programme. The clerk at the other end of the line seemed extremely doubtful about my chances of getting there.

"What, even if we leave immediately?" I asked. "We have at least two hours in which to get there."

"It's possible but highly improbable," the clerk said.

"Don't be fatuous, and send a car round at once," I said and replaced the receiver.

Half an hour was to pass before the car arrived. I spent the time taking a bath and changing into evening clothes, occasionally glancing round to see if my "puffer"—the rubber inhaler—was to hand if required. During my illness I had been taking Ephedrine and Dexadrine, strictly under doctor's order. I now took another dose of these drugs to fortify myself against the evening's stresses. Then, as I waited for the car, I swallowed some more whisky. This cheered me enormously, although the amount I took could not have harmed a curate at a whist drive.

We set off for the studio and, for two-thirds of the way, made fairly good progress. But when we hit a really bad patch of fog I was obliged to get out and walk ahead of the car in order to keep the driver from mounting the pavement. The fog was raw and thick and I swallowed mouthfuls of the vile stuff.

Still, we reached the studio in good time for me to make up and sort myself out. My three days in bed had left me rather weak in the knees and my trudge through the fog had completely chased away the sense of well-being I felt before I set out. Another whisky might have set me up, but I refused to have one when offered. I felt light-headed with fatigue and exhaustion. The only normal thing about me, just then, was my flaming temper. Feeling completely done in, I quietly cursed myself for being foolish enough to leave my bed.

Everyone else seemed to be equally "under the weather." Apparently the programme went wrong from the start. The white line that normally unfolds on the viewers' screens under the opening caption came on as a short dash. Then it stuck altogether, due to a film break.

I guessed the occupation of one of the challengers, an income-tax inspector. Before he left I complimented him, saying: "I have met two gentlemen of your occupation in my life. One was very pleasant and the other very unpleasant. You are one of the nice ones."

After ten minutes the intense heat of the lighting had its inevitable effect and I just folded up. No celebrity turned up for the quiz blind spot. So Eamonn Andrews took the celebrity's chair after we were blind-folded. He began to address us in a piping voice which I found extremely difficult to hear.

When it was my turn to ask questions I said: "I will if I can make myself heard over the boisterous audience." In his own voice, Eamonn said reprovingly: "The very small studio audience."

Finally, at the end of the programme, the roller caption which announces the names of the panel appeared crookedly on the screen. And I walked crookedly to my car and went crookedly home to bed.

The next morning I battled against a temperature of 102 degrees and a never silent telephone. Telegrams of sympathy poured in. Well-wishers sent asthma cures, cough mixtures, parcels of food. Some time during the morning Cecil McGivern

199

came to see me. He sat beside the bed, discussed the show and was very sympathetic and charming. It did not need a doctor's eye to convince him, or anyone else, that I was ill and that it was bad luck that I had ever left my bed to take part in the programme.

Although the B.B.C. generously explained that I was a very sick man, the publicity which this incident attracted was extremely painful to me. When I again left my sick bed to keep a promise to speak at a Jewish discussion circle in Streatham, the press gleefully reported me out of context as saying: "We must have a settled determination not to lose our temper about things which do not matter."

I became increasingly upset about the attention which was being paid to every move I made. One paper cynically headed reports on my activities "Gilbert Harding—Day by Day." Letters of criticism poured in. Vile letters. Abusive letters. Many of them anonymous. Early the following year I offered my resignation to the TV chiefs. But Cecil McGivern said: "Ignore the attacks on you. We want you in the show."

So I struggled on. Badly though I needed a holiday, I retained my seat on the panel, and saw the thing through till the summer of 1953, when the B.B.C. decided to give the whole thing a rest. Apart from one major rumpus—when I was allegedly rude to the ventriloquist's dummy, Archie Andrews—I managed to keep my temper. Relatively speaking.

21

I AM tempted to call these final chapters How Not to be a
Celebrity. What *is* a Celebrity? I do not know. As for myself,
I am a weary middle-aged man in need of a good rest, a long
holiday away from public life. Yet when I was ill with 'flu
recently I chafed and fretted, watched the clock, and longed to
be out and about. Action has become a habit with me. Because
I am a more ill-tempered man than most, I am a very bad
patient. It would be different in hospitals, with nurses, for they
are so considerate and efficient. But to be in one's own bed,
dependent on the affectionate but futile attentions of friends is
irksome.

As I lay there, I thought bitterly of the shams and pre-
tensions of public life—especially when one has earned one's
notoriety through the phoney media of sound radio and
Television. Just before I went sick I had received two radio
"Oscars." One, a silver screen for TV, I shared with Richard
Dimbleby, but the other, a silver microphone for sound radio
I had all to myself. Under no illusions as to what is, and what
is not, "outstanding" in regard to a radio personality, I was
both touched and dispirited by these acquisitions. What a
flimsy way to earn a public reputation! The only real satisfaction I got was the realization that there are people who do
not expect one to "smarm" all the time, and try to ingratiate
oneself with every stranger who claps one on the back and
says: "You don't know me, but I know you. Now listen——"

Somehow I find myself engaged in a constant struggle
to fight off bores. No one likes people, or cherishes friend-
ships, more than I do. But one must have limits. Life today
is bad enough with its intolerable delays at telephone exchanges,
and on railways, with broken promises to deliver coal and oil,

with newspapers arriving so late you have no time to read them and letters being delivered later every day—life is complicated enough, I say, without having to take on the woes and burdens of complete strangers as well.

Then there is the notion that I am a vast repository of knowledge. One third of my letters ask me such questions as: Who is Mattli? Who were the sons of Zebedee? I now have a stock answer for these presumptuous people—consult your local librarian.

It is usually disastrous to accept requests from strangers to meet you. They invariably come out of curiosity and then bore you to tears by telling you their miserable life stories. Or of how ambitious they are, and how easy things would be if you brought them to the attention of the Director-General of the B.B.C. or Sir Winston Churchill. Whenever I have managed to find people jobs I have heard no more from them, except the ones who got sacked who came back for me to find them something else, "perhaps more congenial."

One's telephone jangles with the noise of women who want to marry you, or say that they know your family, or ask outright for cash. Spiritualists and suchlike knock at the door to tell you they have just been talking to your father. Mothers with gifted and talented daughters ask you to see that they get a chance to appear in Television. Or a man tries to sell you a Picasso and calls you an intellectual nonentity for failing to do so. Since so many of these persons would be only too happy to accuse me of libel, I will not gratify their manias and frustrations by describing any of them.

Notoriety has other strange consequences. People press gifts upon you. Not all spring from altruistic motives. Spectacles, shoes, household goods arrive from time to time; unless one has agreed to endorse these products one must be careful not to make use of them. Recently I was asked to accept a pleasant sum of money to advertise a brand of cigarettes. Then the deal was called off. I learnt that the directors had decided that so many people loathed the sight of me that my endorsement might decrease sales. That amused me. Particularly since other cigarette firms were doing their best to persuade me to endorse their particular brands.

To add to my catalogue of crimes committed in the cause of what is called entertainment I recently made a gramophone record with that delightful and talented woman, Hermione Gingold. Rehearsals were exhausting, but we managed to produce a spirited duet called *It Takes Two to Tango*. On the other side I played wolf to Hermione's Red Riding Hood. The words for this second tune were written by Annette Mills, creator of Muffin the Mule! Then the B.B.C. decided we had gone too far, and the record was banned. What nonsense that was! The song was far less suggestive than most of the awful, moony sex lyrics imported from the U.S.A. I suppose I should have recorded a learned discourse on life's profundities.

There was also some tut-tutting among my more sensitive friends when I appeared in a comic show on Television with Frankie Howerd. Yet Frankie is a fine artist and—after all—*What's My Line?* is not exactly a highbrow show. Yet people constantly deplore what they call my "lapses" into light entertainment. The best light entertainers I have ever known were the late Cyril Joad and my dear friend Sir Compton Mackenzie!

As a result of these incursions into "showmanship" my life has now become quite bizarre. I am plagued by cranks and pestered by crackpots who regard me as an information bureau, employment exchange and banker. Who do they think they are, these so-called fans who ask me to introduce them to Danny Kaye, arrange free trips to America, get them free tickets for the latest American musical show? I dislike them intensely.

I distrust all begging letters and do nothing about them. On the other hand, I will give what I can spare to people who are down on their luck or in need, if they come my way. Not long ago a battered old woman in broken-down shoes stopped me in the street and asked for a shilling. I took her home, gave her eggs in milk and a whisky and a pound note. Was that so unusual? Yet when I told a friend about my ancient guest, he shook his head disapprovingly. I thoroughly enjoyed the old lady's company—which is more than I can say of some of her grander sisters.

Another form of duplicity is the autograph hunter's trick of saying, "It's not for me, but for my son." Or niece. Or favourite aunt. The other day a woman approached me in a club where I happened to be finishing a piece of cold chicken before taking part in a Ladies' Night brains trust. Elizabeth Allan and I had agreed to go along without payment for the amusement and edification of this woman and her friends.

"Can I have your autograph?" she asked brusquely, thrusting a crumpled piece of paper under my nose.

"When I've finished my supper, certainly," I said.

"Oh, don't think I'm one of your fans," the woman shrilled. "I only want you to sign this for a friend."

"Then why bother if you dislike me so much?" I asked.

"Oh, you nasty rude man!" she replied.

"Madam," I said, "if I wanted any lessons in rudeness I would go to you for them. Now do you mind if I finish my supper?"

Later that evening the woman's husband came up to me and complained that I had been rude to his wife!

With some difficulty I can understand children wanting people to sign their names in a book. These things are part of a child's life, conditioned by habit and environment, like stamp collecting or hoarding conkers. But it baffles me when I find adults producing scraps of paper and old envelopes and clamouring for the signature of those who are supposed to be celebrated.

I don't know who it was who said that "the best things in life are free." I do remember, however, that my grandfather used to counter all my requests for money to go to the pictures or to buy sweets with the suggestion that a glass of water and a good country walk would be very much better for me. Now,

I do not see much harm (no matter how exasperating it can be) in being asked by people one has never met and will never see again, to scribble one's name for them. That costs nothing. What does cost a lot is to answer innumerable letters and to acknowledge the receipt of suggestions from people who seem to have unlimited leisure at their disposal and a curious disregard for other people's patience and pocket.

I am still hoping to find the courage to refuse to answer any letter which asks for information, for photographs and for tickets to radio shows, unless the writer sends a stamped and addressed envelope. Some of my colleagues who, like myself, have acquired some form of public prominence, attend to this matter cheerfully and with a good will. I do not. Most of these correspondents only want to make some sort of capital out of their pretentious approaches.

I despise the cowardly senders of "chain of good luck" letters, and wish all the ill luck to these monsters who threaten serious injury or even death if I do not pass such letters on. In answering casual letters, in the attempt to give manifestly useless information, there lies little reward except the negative satisfaction of feeling that at least one has taken the trouble to write to one.

Then there is the "public appearance." I now find that my grandfather's dictum on the pleasures of all things that are free to be false, or at best a half truth. I find that the things one does not get paid for are infinitely more exasperating and annoying, more irritating and unrewarding than the "engagements" which carry a fee—however small.

I am not unduly modest, but I always have an uncomfortable feeling that when I am asked to open a Methodist bazaar in the Midlands or an Episcopalian fête in Argyllshire, the organizers are indeed scraping the very bottom of the barrel. I have also found that when one gets to these places (and sometimes one does) one's arrival and presence are all that matters. Responsibility for one's convenience or entertainment is in no one's hands. One just makes a dreary round of the stalls, buying unwanted things for more than one can really afford to pay—then the limp handshake, "How good of you to come—you can find the way to the station, can't you?"

Recently I was asked to go to take part in some function to do with child guidance and happy marriage. When I wrote (at my own expense) to say that, being unmarried and childless, I felt that my views would be worthless, the organizer telephoned to me early the following morning to denounce me for my unmarried and childless state, and to tell me that my letter "just didn't make sense." Am I to be exposed to this kind of rudeness because the B.B.C. asks me, perhaps far too often, to broadcast?

A woman rang me up to ask me to "christen" a monkey. I said I would do nothing of the kind—and said so with some acerbity. Christen, indeed! What next? But there came a sharp note of rebuke to me for my insolence and ill-temper, for which, since the rebuke was well-founded, I felt I had to apologize. More time wasted, more money (however little) spent, in bearing the burden of notoriety.

If only one had been born in a "dark, unfathomed cave of ocean"! Oh, for the desert air on which to waste one's sweetness!

No sooner is the summer spate of garden parties over, than the Christmas bazaars begin, with more demands that I should contribute a few words to set the selling in motion. Ministers of every denomination and charitable organizers of every kind invite me to the four corners of this island. Presumably they want to attract people who will come to see if I really am as grotesque as I look and sound.

To maintain some sanity, I have worked out a rationing system. Three a week of these bazaars and fêtes and no more.

22

JUST to keep myself busy, I became a newspaper "columnist." Thus, many years after I had gone round Fleet Street looking for journalistic work, I found myself working at high pressure for a leading Sunday newspaper.

It started when I was challenged by the radio critic of that newspaper to "really do something" instead of just complaining about the way things were. To prove that I was not simply an old humbug who would not raise a finger to put things right, I replied that my broadcast remarks were not based on high falutin' philosophy but from a close observation of the life around me. So I was offered the facilities of the paper to investigate and report the injustices and scandals of the nation.

I quickly went into action. I read what reports and letters I could and organized expert help where needed. Then I began to follow-up some of the cases. My first journey was to the mud flats beyond Ilford, Essex, where I had heard of the plight of a young married couple who lived on a tiny wooden houseboat, so gimcrack that their children lived with relations at Ilford and only joined them at week-ends.

As I splashed through the mud to this derelict looking home I thought grimly that a reporter's life is not for middle-aged, asthmatic men, but when I reached my destination and clambered aboard I also understood the reporter's rare moments of reward for the harassed life he leads. The place was an eyesore, and after interviewing the couple, a Mr. and Mrs. McBane, I called at the Ilford Housing Committee to draw their attention to this scandal. I found the Committee helpful, and left feeling that the McBanes would be looked after.

Between broadcasting dates I would find myself travelling throughout the country, interviewing, probing, writing as I went. It was far more hectic than any of my travels for *Round Britain Quiz*, but also more stimulating. I really did find myself getting closer to other people's problems than ever before.

The winter was well advanced when I started this job, and I coughed and wheezed my way into people's homes, listening to their problems. Though many considered me an old busybody, I did get things moving.

One chilly afternoon I found myself trudging down the muddy lane leading to the smallholding of Mr. Stanley List, at Shipdam, Norfolk. List had written me an account of his troubles which he described as "appalling." They were indeed. He lived with his wife and three children at the end of the narrow, slushy trail from the main road.

Soon the harassed father was pouring out his troubles—how the authorities refused to make up the lane and how he had been taken to court three times for not sending his children nearly two miles to school during the bad weather. Even the dustmen refused to take away his rubbish because of the state of the lane.

Then Mr. List showed me a letter from the local council saying: "It is impossible to give sanitary service until reasonable means of access is provided."

"About the children," I said. "I thought schools provided transport for school children in remote areas. Why not yours?"

"Because," said Mr. List, "we do not live more than two miles from the school. They came and measured the distance to my door and found that it was only one and three-quarter miles—and eighty-five yards!"

"That spirit can go to blazes," I thought. "They refuse to mend the man's lane, then refuse to send the dustcart down it because it is in such a bad state. They refuse to collect his children for school, and haul him into court when he fails to get them there in bad weather." Off I went to a local telephone box and got through to the clerk of the local council.

I said: "Has it ever occurred to you to put down a few loads of granite chippings and then run a steam-roller over them?"

The official explained that nothing could be done until the Norfolk County Council took over the lane—and they would not do that unless the landowners did some of the work.

"More passing the buck," I said, hanging up.

Then I telephoned the county education officer about the children. This gentleman said he was fairly new to his job and had not yet heard of the case.

"You soon will, my dear sir, you soon will," I replied.

Next I spoke to the regional officer of medical health.

"It's a terrible place," I said. "Have you a welfare officer who could go and see it? That family should not be living there at all."

The M.O. promised to look into it but pointed out that there were other families in a similar plight in Norfolk. I filed the papers for further enquiry and then set off for the Cambridgeshire village of Little Wratting to take up the grievance of the villagers who had been trying for months to get a pillar box for themselves! I got on to the area postmaster and that afternoon he sent a man to investigate.

These things may sound trivial, but to me they justified all I had said publicly and privately about official bumble-dom and the awful attitude of people who, through shyness or class inhibitions, failed to speak up for themselves. Altogether I must have seen about a hundred cases. Not all were justifiable grievances, and I did not succeed in righting every wrong. But I did kick up an unholy rumpus wherever I went and that did a certain amount of good. If only people would speak up for their rights!

For weeks I sat in my office near Covent Garden, fuming against officials and civil servants all over the country. I had experts available to give technical and legal help, but I personally investigated cases of outstanding injustice.

For one week, despite "Housewives' Choice" broadcasts

every morning I darted off to distant parts to distribute gift parcels to families as far apart as Ludlow, on the Welsh border, and Sheffield. I also found time to dress up as Santa Claus and hand out small gifts to some extremely nice and polite children in the London area. Not my favourite role; but the experience has made me feel for the poor men who impersonate Father Christmas in the stores during those frantic weeks of shopping.

I could not stop investigations by the police who have a vital public function to perform. I could not compel employers to take back discharged workers. That is always a matter for the employer and organizations such as trade unions. I could not build ships to take people to Australia, South Africa or Timbuctoo. But I could make myself heard above the polite rattle of civil service teacups, and I revelled in my job.

Above all, I found that the most widespread grievance needing urgent attention by the authorities was—and still is—Housing. The housing situation in Britain is appalling and in my journeys I saw things that were altogether disgraceful and a standing reproach to us all. For a country with our damp climate, we are altogether crudely and miserably housed. And the powers-that-be, who encourage thousands of people to build their own homes by allowing them building materials, then stupidly prevent them from completing the job. There was one case of a man who had built his house up to the top of the wall and then could not put the roof on because of some licensing muddle. I raised the roof about that one.

Then I was suddenly called in to cover my biggest newspaper assignment. This had nothing to do with grievances and chips upon the shoulder. In fact, at the time, it wiped out everything else. This was the funeral of King George VI. There was no place at Windsor for me with the B.B.C.—Broadcasting House did not call on me at all—so I went for my editor, and was moved to the edge of tears.

The flowers touched me most of all as a people's tribute

to a beloved king. And among the great throng of people I felt the drama of those doing homage to a king who would be grievously missed. At the close, I watched the Queen Mother make her deep curtsey of farewell to the open vault. It was then that the tears almost pushed into my eyes. I shall never forget this final gesture of a Royal mourner.

Yet I could not suppress the fact in my report that some of those responsible for conducting this momentous ceremonial came near to marring it. The wondrously beautiful language of the service was sometimes tortured almost out of recognition. Mistakes in reading the sacred texts were made even by one or two of the highest dignitaries. Words were slurred over. There was too much mumbling. Spendid passages suffered severe damage from false stresses and untutored delivery.

It distressed me that, for an occasion designed to impress on millions the high significance of the passing of a monarch, the clergy and ceremonial officers had not all learned by heart, and practised perfect enunciation of, the glorious language they were called upon to pronounce.

All this I duly reported. To my surprise and pain, I found readers resented my critical reporting and there was a great outcry against my having gone to Windsor at all. Once again I found that people seem to prefer rose-tinted half-truths to the facts, and anyone who like myself blurts them out must take the consequences of outraged society.

By this time I found that my own troubles were enough, without chasing about the country looking after those of other people. So while the newspaper continues to serve its readers with expert advice and help, I was assigned to writing a week by week account of what I had seen and heard on my rounds. I had acquired a certain amount of facility, and I continue to produce my weekly column. Sometimes, though, I find myself wondering how much Fleet Street would be interested in the former *Times* correspondent at Cyprus if he gave up his broadcasting, film and other activities. The trouble about freelance broadcasting is that one becomes a thing of shreds and patches—living without pattern.

Housing was one of my chief problems. My time-table was so full that I could no longer make the daily train journey to and from Twickenham, where I continued to live with my sister, Constance. So I moved into a furnished ground floor flat off Knightsbridge, near Hyde Park Corner. It was pleasant to be within a few minutes' taxi ride of most of the B.B.C. studios. While I did not think highly of the furniture, for a while it seemed an improvement on the rather cramped quarters I had shared so long with my sister. Constance continued to live at Twickenham, and sometimes Mother would come up from Hereford and stay with her there.

Matters were not improved for me by the almost morbid curiosity my presence would attract wherever I went. In the remotest country pub I would find myself being prodded and examined as if I was some visitation from another planet, and my ears would be afflicted by that now dreadfully familiar opening gambit: "You don't know me but I know you."

I had also acquired some sort of a reputation for rudeness, which, though unjustified, provoked extraordinary outbursts of rudeness against me. Now I feel very strongly about this. Up and down the country there may be waiters, railway attendants and hotel janitors to whom I have undoubtedly been outspoken. But this must not be confused with rudeness. It is rudeness to be deliberately unkind to anyone or to make personal remarks about others' appearance, accent or origin.

It is rude not to ask others if you may smoke while they are still eating or not to offer seats to elderly or heavily laden women. (Young women can stand up, so far as I am concerned.) It is rude not to say "please" and "thank you" for everything. But it is not rude to say "what" instead of "pardon."

Far from being rude myself, I find that I am living in an age when rudeness abounds. In that category I place the M.P. who once sat for an English University. I was once with him in a barber's shop and we were both waiting our turn when a chair became vacant. He immediately jumped into it and sat down. At this I went to him and said:

"I think it is my turn."

To this he replied: "How can that possibly matter?"

I may have my own code of courtesy and I cannot pretend to be tongue-tied when it is challenged. The legend that I am rude is rivalled only by the legend that I hate women. I have always enjoyed the company of a witty or gracious woman, but there again it is perhaps my inability to "smarm" that usually keeps them at a distance. I think that most of the so-called "great lovers" must have been awful liars at heart.

What is ridiculous is for a young man to deliberately set out to become a bachelor. I met such a one recently. He was suffering all the agonies of lovesickness and complained: "I've fallen in love with a girl and it makes me feel such a fool."

"How old are you?" I asked, and his surprising answer was, "Old enough to know better—twenty-three."

My reply was: "Then you are a fool—and a bigger one than you think. There are no circumstances—job, career or money —to excuse a healthy young man for avoiding marriage."

That I believe, though I also think it is nonsense to say that at my age it is never too late to change one's bachelor state. It isn't much fun having a son or daughter of twenty when you are well over sixty yourself, although in my case there are other reasons that, so far as I can see, will keep me from marrying.

Apart from Hermione Gingold, I think the woman who endeared herself most to me during the past few years was a complete stranger. I had gone for a short holiday to the seaside with my mother. As I was sitting on a bench looking at the sea and trying to relax, the woman stopped and, glaring at me, said:

"Ugly man, ugly woman."

"Really, madame," I replied, "the ugly man being myself, I presume?"

"Certainly," she said.

"And," I added, "the ugly woman being you?"

"Of course," she said, and tripped off.

It occurred to me afterwards that perhaps she had hoped we could have made a true marriage there on the spot. Soon after I moved into my new flat in the summer of 1952 I found that it was not so pleasant after all. Though I had escaped from the Twickenham place with its screeching main road, howling aeroplanes leaving the airports, and noisy neighbours, the drabness of the furniture and thinness of the walls soon began to wear down my patience. Much of this has been written between those drab walls, with their hideous papering and atrocious pictures, but I hope shortly to move elsewhere. Who knows, perhaps one day I shall really find a home of my own, furnished the way I like and in a perfectly peaceful setting?

Meanwhile, though life has been full of upsets and irritations, it has had its good moments. I never cease to wonder at the kindness and patience of my friends, and also the many spontaneous kindnesses of complete strangers. My position as a public notoriety has granted me certain privileges, and taken me into many spheres of life, which would have been denied me had I remained content with my lot as a schoolmaster. While I sometimes hanker for a quiet life away from the headlines, for a pensionable job which keeps me occupied from morning till evening in the office, shop or factory, I know I have become what I am because of restlessness and my inability to stay harnessed down for long to anything, or anyone.

Life remains full of surprises. I have even managed to enjoy myself at garden parties and bazaars, thanks to the unexpected encounter or the flawless pleasure of a splendid day, unmarred by stupid incidents.

I remember going to a cricket fête in a charming Essex village. There was no humbug there. Even the licensing laws had relaxed their inhibited humbugism and an enterprising brewery had sent a tent with a beautiful painted inn sign and cheerful men to serve cool beer. A young man studying philosophy at Cambridge ran a gay little gambling joint, which raised pounds and "a grand time was had by all." The vicar, bless him, enjoyed every minute of it—and so did I.

Yet I sometimes wonder if many of these fêtes are really necessary. I myself have turned down invitations to no fewer than seventy-four garden parties and eighteen church fêtes on a single day. Are there enough celebrities to go round? I wonder. And I wonder how many accept the number I do. Few, I should think.

I cannot understand this Hollywood fever to ballyhoo a "name" which has percolated into the most remote vicarages and mothers' unions in the land. It makes me wonder if local ingenuity and local pride are dying, and, flippant though this subject may be, it does show to what lengths the churches have to go to raise funds nowadays.

One of the most worthwhile functions I ever had the honour of attending was a dinner given for Lieutenant "Abbie" Sweetwine, the "coloured" girl from Florida who showed such tremendous courage and fortitude in looking after the victims of the Harrow and Wealdstone train disaster in 1952. At this function more than £7,000 raised by the U.S. Air Force for the National Playing Field Association was presented to General "Boy" Browning, representing the Duke of Edinburgh. I had the great privilege of proposing the health of Lieutenant Sweetwine. This gave me the precious chance to say what I have always said and will go on saying—that people who think they are better than other people only because their noses are a different shape, their skin a different colour or their creeds or language of a different kind are the raw ingredients of Fascism and beastliness.

On another occasion I was asked to broadcast "The Week's Good Cause" on behalf of the Hostel of John for the Dying. The Appeal Secretary told me that we could not expect more than £1,200. I found the appeal very difficult to write and I worried whether I should deliver it effectively, for the cause meant a great deal to me.

In just over four minutes I had to appeal to the generosity

215

of listeners, idling by their sets on a hot August evening. There are so many things to be avoided in broadcasting, since the B.B.C. has always been anxious not to upset people in homes who may be suffering—or have relatives and dear ones suffering—from some ailment the mention of which might be painful. I wrote and re-wrote my piece about fifteen times. The B.B.C., quite rightly, will never allow an appeal to be pre-recorded, so I went along to Broadcasting House conscious that it was up to me to help provide financial support for the hospital's proposed scheme to build a new wing.

John Donne came to my rescue. I ended my brief, but carefully thought out speech, with these lines from one of his finest sonnets:

"Death be not proud, though some have called thee Mighty and dreadful, for, thou art not so."

The appeal raised more than £5,000, enough money to complete the new wing. When the Queen Mother opened it in the summer of 1953 I was presented to her. I very much admired the extraordinary skill with which this most gracious lady found something particular to say to each one of the seventy-five patients in the wing.

During the all too brief time I was in her presence we discussed the extraordinary generosity of people, and I am proud to say Her Majesty agreed with my lifelong contention that there are more pleasant people about than unpleasant.

This account of my life must end here. If I live long enough, perhaps there will be a sequel to it. If not, I can only say that the public owes me two debts of gratitude. First, because I do not drive a car. Second, because I have no children. But I do wish that the future were over.